“The story of the adoptio
by the Kuhls family is ov
the opportunity to meet .

and Ron’s family. The fact that they chose to adopt the child with the greatest needs communicates the deep love that God has placed in the hearts of the two spouses. Looking over the years on Ionut’s reunion with his natural family in Huși, Romania, is a miracle in which God’s providence has manifested itself abundantly.”

Mihai Dumitrascu,
Senior Pastor, Biserica Emmanuel, Galati, Romania

“As one of the pastors in the Kuhls’ church, I had a front-row seat to the story captured in this book. Maybe you wonder if God ever speaks today. Maybe you wonder if God is capable of true healing and wonderful transformation. Noot’s story is a miracle and the living answer to the question of God’s engagement today.

“I remember the first time Noot came walking/running down the church hallway shortly after arriving in the US (before his prosthetic legs had been fitted). He was full of energy, a contagious personality, and unstoppable optimism. As a cross-cultural adoptive parent myself, I fully understand the concerns and fears any adoptive parent walks into with a cross-cultural adoption. Ron and Barb are amazing advocates for God-inspired adoption. Even better, the story is not complete. Noot is continuing to write new chapters in his own journey of faith and engagement. Thank you for sharing your story, and thank you for living out simple courageous faith.”

Ken Nabi, Regional President of Converge Great Lakes

"One woman's incredible dream turns into an incredible reality in this amazing adoption story. God's fingerprints are on display from the beginning to the breathtaking end. The reader will come away fully inspired by a child who began life with an uncertain future and who now soars on wings of eagles."

Kristi Wilkinson, Author, *The Child Who Listens*

Standby *for* GOD

Fearless Flight
Into A Faithful Calling

A SPECIAL NEEDS ADOPTION STORY

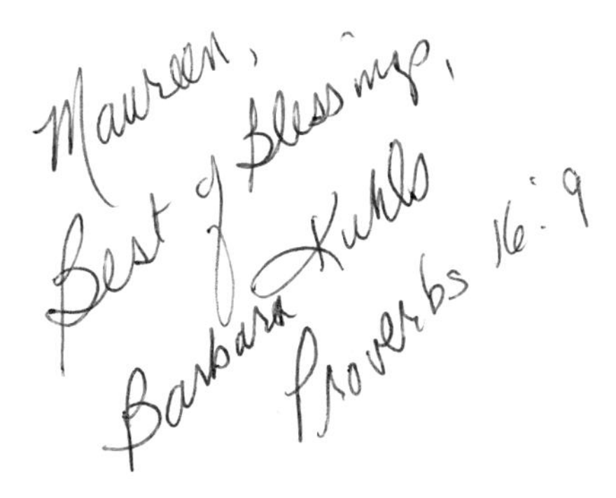

BARBARA KUHLS

AKA My Kid's Mom

Standby for God: Fearless Flight into a Faithful Calling

Print ISBN: 979-8-218-04653-8
Ebook ISBN: 979-8-218-04654-5
Library of Congress: 2022919411

This is a work of nonfiction. The events and experiences described are all true and have been faithfully rendered as I have remembered them to the best of my ability. I have changed the names, identities, and circumstances of some of the people depicted in order to protect their privacy.

Printed in the United States

DEDICATION

This book is dedicated to Christi Andries, husband of Andreea Stoica Andries. Their marriage made possible the reunion of Ionut with his Romanian family of birth.

Proceeds from this book will benefit children with special needs.

CONTENTS

ACKNOWLEDGMENTS

While I never thought of myself as a writer, there is a running narrative in my mind, describing events, relationships, scenes, and my reactions to them. Ever the one to journal, my husband and others occasionally asked, "When are you going to write that book?" What book? These are just my random thoughts between me and God about life. Whenever we told the story of God choosing our third child for us, listeners would say, "You need to write a book!"

When our son reunited with his birth family, we all gained another family. During that reunion, I heard God whisper: "Now. Write the book." If you are reading this, you may be one who encouraged me to write it, so I thank you for that push.

I especially thank my husband Ron for his encouragement and support along the way. Few people know this, but he is the one who generously made a gift to Romanian pastors in 2001. *Reteaua* (Network) *the Participant's Guide* was translated into Romanian for pastors to teach the spiritual gifts to Christ followers from this gift. Bruce L. Bugsby and Bill Hybels wrote the original English version.

Words can't describe how much I appreciate our son Ionut allowing me to share his story so it could encourage others—despite his humility and reluctance to his story becoming public. He has read every chapter and could write many more himself, but that will be another story. I also thank him for the beautiful cover photo taken from one of his many flights. Thank you, Tom Otte, of tomotteimaging.com, for the author photo, making me even better looking than I really am (winking here).

I have deep gratitude and utmost respect for Carmen and Catalin Stoica, who gave Ionut life and continue praying for him. They welcomed us into their family with gratitude that God would return their son as an adult. I hope this blesses them. I owe their daughter, Andreea—much too soon the widow of her beloved husband, Christi Andries—a great debt for reconnecting the families and assisting her parents with their chapter in this book, which is easily the best one.

Multumesc (thank you) to Tamara Neacsu and Ruxandra Neacsu, who have helped us translate over the years. This volume was entirely translated by them into Romanian in order to bless people of their nation with stories of God's goodness in their own heart language. Tavi Iordache, another young interpreter, and his parents, Pastor Eugen and Nicoleta Iordache of Galati, were immensely instrumental in making the reunion happen. They not only hosted us in their home but fed us delicious meals and drove us to Huşi for the wedding and everywhere else we wanted to go. Multumesc to Daniel and Delia Blidar, who warmly welcomed and housed Ionut many times and included him in the larger Romanian congregation of evangelical Christians in Chicagoland. I am also grateful to Pastor Tim Haugen, Pastor Mihai Dumitrascu, Pastor Ken Nabi, Jeanette Stone, and so many other Bible teachers, too numerous to mention, who have been personally instrumental in guiding me on the journey of life as a Christ follower.

A huge thank you to Shriner's Hospital for Children and Scheck & Siress Prosthetics for outfitting and maintaining Noot's "Shriner Feet." Marty Ryan also deserves a shout-out for his devoted care and maintenance for keeping Noot on his feet. I also thank the many teachers and therapists who were instrumental in making Ionut an American, speaking and reading our language, and adjusting to our weird culture.

Kristi Wilkinson, whose book *The Child Who Listens* was placed in my hands, has been a tremendous cheerleader and pre-editor for this project. She has become a dear friend who is also an adoptive mother of a Romanian son. I am indebted to her and hope to meet her in person soon. I must thank Susan Baganz, author and friend, who led by example and encouraged me to continue. Beth Lottig, my editor and publisher, has turned my rough manuscript into something you found worthy of reading. Thanks, Beth.

The Tuesday Brigade, Garage Galz, and many other friends prayed me through this project. I am thankful for each and every one of you who believed in me and took all the details to the throne. Bless you, Mary Tighe, for allowing me to use your place for uninterrupted writing.

Being a lifelong reader, I appreciate the multitude of authors whose books I have read. If I have borrowed a phrase or style from any of their works, I apologize, as it was not intentional. What I read weaves into the fiber of my brain, not allowing me to sort original thoughts from those of others. My brain includes fibers from books, poetry, music, history textbooks, magazines, and any other literature that comes before my eyes. I thank my mom, Dorothy, for teaching me and inspiring me to read for information, pleasure, and challenge. I thank my English teachers, who taught me spelling, vocabulary, grammar, and creative expression.

Most of all, I thank my heavenly Father, who adopted me when I was fatherless. By His grace and love, He received me into His royal family and has given me all that I need and much more than I could ever have desired or imagined. Without His love and the sacrifice of His Son Jesus, my redeemer, this book would not be in your hands, for it would not have come from my life to the keyboard. His book, the Holy Bible, is by far the best one I read over and over. You need to pick it up and read it as soon as you put this one down.

But when the set time had fully come, God sent his Son, born of a woman, born under the law, to redeem those under the law, that we might receive adoption to sonship. Because you are his sons, God sent the Spirit of his Son into our hearts, the Spirit who calls out, "Abba, Father." So you are no longer a slave, but God's child; and since you are his child, God has made you also an heir.

GALATIANS 4:4–7

DARK TIMES

Nicolae Ceaușescu had decimated the economy along with the spirit of most Romanians with his tightfisted communist regime. While he taxed and overtaxed the workers, he was building for himself an extravagant palace in Bucharest. He wanted this to be the largest, most opulent building in the world. He purchased (seized) homes in the area for pennies from multiple city blocks to make room for his palace. Marble and gold covered the walls, floors, and grand stairways to rooms large enough for several families' tiny homes. He also purchased homes not required for the footprint of the palace for lei (pennies) and then rented them back to the people for thousands. It was Ceaușescu's greedy way of owning and controlling everything and everyone. Most had no choice but to live in ugly square apartment buildings made of cement blocks. These were up to ten stories high with no working elevators.

In Iasi and other cities, these buildings were "heated" by the government. A giant central boiler for heat was the source of heat for buildings up to three blocks away. Giant pipes carried the heated air through the frigid winter air to the people's apartments, losing large amounts of the heat along the way. Those who were rich enough to live close to the heating plant had to open their windows to tolerate the excess, while those at the fringes kept their coats on indoors. Sometimes there was water warm enough for a shower, but one could not rely on it.

During these years of communism, working people could afford only one child or two—if any. Ceaușescu assured them their babies would be well-fed in government orphanages while parents waited in lines with ration cards to purchase food, which was often not even available. In truth, his goal was to indoctrinate and train them in communism, so they would be good soldiers. Boys were preferred, although athletic girls were acceptable too.

On December 25, 1989, the people rose up and demanded an end to his madness. For days, throngs of citizens filled the square surrounding his palace. Finally, the madman was tried and executed—communism was collapsing!

As foreigners began to penetrate the borders for relief and recovery, his orphanages were exposed. Children were found malnourished, sickly, uneducated, and living in worse conditions than American animals. Many had already been turned out onto the streets to beg for survival.

Christians and good-hearted people from Sweden, Italy, the USA, and other Western countries gradually took over the orphanages and started new ones. Parents who could reclaimed their children, but for most, it was too late. They could not be found. Caretakers, also known as mamas, did the best they could, but food and supplies were still hard to come by for so many little ones.

DREAM A NEW DREAM

In the Spring of 1997, I responded to the cries of a baby, going to the crib to see what the little one needed. There he was, wrapped in a blanket with his tiny feet inside booties—but not attached to his body. Startled, I realized I had been dreaming. Knowing that God does speak to people in dreams, I wondered about this dream's meaning.

"Father God," I prayed, "If this is you telling me something, please explain, for I am confused. Yet, if it is not from you, help me to forget, for this is quite strange."

Several days later, while at my desk working for Bethany Christian Services, I was stunned once again. As a birth parent counselor, I did not often read the notices and emails pertaining to the caseworkers assigned to screen and assist adoptive parents. Not wanting to be emotionally drawn to their stories, I preferred to focus on the needs and process of birth parents who were making adoption plans. Not remarkably busy that day, however, I allowed myself to peruse the list entitled "Children of a Promise." These were children and infants who were cleared for adoption but were more difficult to place in families due to their age and special needs.

Scanning the list, I noticed sibling groups, older children from foreign countries, and those with minor to severe medical needs. The last one on the list caught my attention, and I reread the description of a two-year-old boy born in Romania with only one hand and no feet. Instantly, I recalled my dream a few days earlier and knew that God was telling me something—but what?

Surely, He was not suggesting that my husband Ron and I adopt him. We were already in our forties with two grown children—one already married and the other living on his own. Starting over would be ludicrous, not to mention this child would have more than a few special needs. Again, I was startled, so I got up to discuss it with my administrative assistant and friend, Ann Haugen, the only other person there.

"Oh, my word!" was all that Ann could say. After she thought about it for a bit, she wisely suggested, "We should pray."

I agreed. "That's it!" Although I already knew in my spirit but was not ready to consider it, I ventured, "God wants us to pray for this little tyke to be placed with parents that will love and take care of him, providing the environment he will need to grow into the purpose God has for him." So together, we prayed. And I silently promised God I would pray for him whenever he came to mind.

I would not yet mention it to Ron. Considering that he would often get me anything I showed any interest in, I did not want his thoughts to go in that direction. At least not yet. I was not sure I wanted this and was not about to bring it to pass by talking or even thinking about it. In fact, the whole notion was scaring me half to death.

I got back to work and tried to focus on current cases. I had a birth mom to meet with the following day and a TPR hearing at the end of the week. A Termination of Parental Rights is not only very emotional for a birth mother but also requires a great deal of detailed legal paperwork from the caseworker.

Only a few weeks went by, and a new issue of *Lifelines*, the quarterly magazine for Bethany, arrived. I enjoyed reading the articles that inspired me. Oftentimes, I learned to relate more to the adoptive parents and better understand the birth parents and adoptees. I usually made time to pray for the "Children of a Promise," whose pictures were featured in a regular section. Once again, God got my attention when I noticed a picture of the exact same child that had been in my dream! His face looked so sad and lonely. The brief description provided a name, his city, and his date of birth. Silently whispering a prayer, I just knew that God would find him suitable parents, and I felt privileged to be a part of His work.

I had witnessed dozens of miracles from the front row in the drama of adoption.

For now God does speak—now one way, now another—though no one perceives it. In a dream, in a vision of the night, when deep sleep falls upon people as they slumber in their beds.

Job 33:14–15

STANDBY FOR THYROID

Later that spring, my husband, Ron, noticed a small lump in his throat. A series of tests and an appointment with Dr. Alison, an ENT (ear, nose, throat specialist), revealed thyroid cancer. Anytime cancer is mentioned concerning your own health or that of a loved one, it can be upsetting, to say the least. There is always a great deal to absorb and process. Dr. Alison assured us by saying, "If you are going to get cancer, this is the type you want to get. Surgery will remove it, and it does not metastasize. It will not come back."

My thoughts were, "I am to focus on my husband and his needs and health. Obviously, God is not preparing us for parenthood again." Yet, I was also reading in 2 Kings chapter 20, where Hezekiah asked for fifteen more years, so he could raise his son. God granted his prayer.

Dr. Alison suggested a biopsy to determine the specific type of thyroid cancer this was. Ron—not liking hospitals or anything to do with medical care—asked if they could just do the surgery to remove it, then determine the type through the pathology of the tumor. That was acceptable to the surgeon, so it was scheduled within a week.

During this summer, Ron continued working. His recovery went smoothly, and he required no chemotherapy, allowing him to continue with life. Medication replaced his thyroid hormone and was relatively easy to regulate. In a follow-up appointment, Dr. Alison assured him that he was cancer-free and could enjoy a long, healthy life. At that point, I recalled that God answered Hezekiah's prayer to give him fifteen more years.

In early September, Ron and I were driving to Platteville, Wisconsin, to attend his grandmother's funeral. We often used the "windshield time" to discuss our jobs and other things. I was telling him about one of the birth moms, a client of mine. This young woman had a six-year-old little boy that the county was removing from her custody. Her history of abusive boyfriends was putting him at risk. Her social worker was encouraging her to make an adoption plan for him before the county intervened and made all the decisions without her input.

"We could adopt him," Ron offered.

"Wait, what?"

"We could adopt him," Ron responded.

Sensing the time was right to inform him of my dream and the picture in *Lifelines*, I recounted it to him.

"Now, I'm confused; which one are you talking about?"

"Both," I said, naively thinking the six-year-old boy would be helpful with the little fellow with all the special needs.

"OK, hold on here. If any of this is from God, we should obey. But if we are just jumping into such a big commitment on emotions, we could have an Ishmael on our hands." He was, of course, making a biblical reference to Abraham and Sarah getting ahead of God and devising their own plan for a son. "If this is from God," he continued, "wouldn't He tell me too?"

That made sense to me, knowing that God prepares a wife's heart but then directs a husband to lead with his head.

"If God wants us to adopt either or both of these kids, he will send me a letter," Ron said matter-of-factly.

Relieved, I agreed. The last time I checked, God was not sending anyone letters. We agreed we would continue to pray for both boys.

Thus says the Lord, the God of David your father: I have heard your prayer; I have seen your tears. Behold, I will heal you . . . and I will add fifteen years to your life."

2 Kings 20:5–6, ESV

LETTER FROM GOD

Ron, not one to pray aloud often, was focused on driving. Not being in the habit of praying together, it was mutually understood that each would pray whenever prompted to do so. We didn't even discuss it. I chose to wait until further direction from Ron. In the meantime, I knew God was finding a forever family for this child.

God was swift in answering. On September 21, 1997, God spoke to us through His Word and our pastor. Tim Haugen preached from 2 Samuel Chapter 9, exhorting believers to care for one another as we are all part of the family of God. This passage was printed as a one-page insert in the church bulletin:

> *David's Kindness to Mephibosheth*
>
> And David said, "Is there still anyone left of the house of Saul, that I may show him kindness for Jonathan's sake?" Now there was a servant of the house of Saul whose name was Ziba, and they called

him to David. And the king said to him, "Are you Ziba?" And he said, "I am your servant." And the king said, "Is there not still someone of the house of Saul, that I may show the kindness of God to him?" Ziba said to the king, "There is still a son of Jonathan; *he is crippled in his feet.*"

The king said to him, "Where is he?" And Ziba said to the king, "He is in the house of Machir the son of Ammiel, at Lo-debar." Then King David sent and brought him from the house of Machir the son of Ammiel, at Lo-debar. And Mephibosheth the son of Jonathan, son of Saul, came to David and fell on his face and paid homage. And David said, "Mephibosheth!" And he answered, "Behold, I am your servant." And David said to him, "Do not fear, for I will show you kindness for the sake of your father Jonathan, and I will restore to you all the land of Saul your father, and you shall eat at my table always." And he paid homage and said, "What is your servant, that you should show regard for a dead dog such as I?"

Then the king called Ziba, Saul's servant, and said to him, "All that belonged to Saul and to all his house I have given to your master's grandson. And you and your sons and your servants shall till the land for him and shall bring in the produce, that your master's grandson may have bread to eat. But Mephibosheth your master's grandson shall always eat at my table." Now Ziba had

> fifteen sons and twenty servants. Then Ziba said to the king, "According to all that my lord the king commands his servant, so will your servant do." So Mephibosheth ate at David's table, like one of the king's sons. And Mephibosheth had a young son, whose name was Mica. And all who lived in Ziba's house became Mephibosheth's servants. So Mephibosheth lived in Jerusalem, for he ate always at the king's table. Now *he was lame in both his feet.*"
> —2 Samuel 9:1–13 (ESV, emphasis mine)

Pastor Tim explained that God adopted us into His family, and we, too, need to "show kindness for the sake of our Father." He reminded the congregation that we would never be alone, calming any fears we had of being less than prepared or "too old" to be parents. The Church, or the family of God, would be there to help and support us. Just as David was honoring his loyalty to his friend Jonathan because they had the same heavenly Father, we as believers need to be willing to do likewise.

After church, Ron turned to me with a stunned expression, wondering if I'd spoken with the pastor about my dream, suggesting we talk to Pastor Tim. We lingered as others departed, then Ron asked to speak to him privately. For the first time, I shared my dream with our pastor. Then Ron described his request for a letter from God. Stunned, the pastor agreed that, indeed, God was speaking to us. He led us in prayer to surrender to God's will before we left his office.

God knew our ability to quickly dismiss his directive, however. Just in case we would do that, He sent another letter. Driving home from church, I noticed a sign indicating a rummage sale at a small rural school that was closing. Restless at home, thinking more about the possibility of actually adopting this child, I decided to get my mind off it for a while and go to that rummage sale. Wanting nothing that a school might have but curious about the inside of James Otis School, I thought it would be a good excuse to explore the little building I often passed.

After a quick exploration of the two classrooms, a small kitchen full of typical student items, desks, books, and other miscellaneous items, I turned to go. About to leave the building, I stopped to read a framed poster next to the exit door. The poster featured the poem "Heaven's Very Special Child" by Edna Mae Massimilla.

"Heaven's Very Special Child"
by Edna Massimilla

A meeting was held quite far from Earth
It was time again for another birth.
Said the Angels to the Lord above—
This special child will need much love.

Her progress may be very slow,
Accomplishment she may not show.
And she'll require extra care
From the folks she meets down there.

She may not run or laugh or play,
Her thoughts may seem quite far away.
So many times she will be labeled
Different, helpless, and disabled.

So, let's be careful where she's sent.
We want her life to be content.
Please, Lord, find the parents who
Will do a special job for you.

They will not realize right away
The leading role they are asked to play.
But with this child sent from above
Comes stronger faith and richer love.

And soon they'll know the privilege given
In caring for their gift from heaven.
Their precious charge, so meek and mild
Is heaven's very special child.[1]

OK, already! I get it! Father, I will do as you ask.

Taking five steps back toward the cashier, I asked, "Is that sign for sale?"

"Sure, why not? What will you give us for it?" asked the man overseeing the estate sale.

"Ten dollars."

He got up to remove the sign, which had been screwed to the wall.

When I showed it to Ron, we were both still shocked that God had sent His letter so quickly—and not one, but two of them!

Now it would be time to get more information from Bethany Christian Services.

Pure and genuine religion in the sight of God
the Father means caring for orphans.

JAMES 1:27, NLT

[1] Used by permission of the copyright holder, Joan Massimilla Pascucci.

BREAKING IT TO OUR KIDS

I did not waste any time calling my supervisor on Monday morning. Donna was the state director of Bethany in Wisconsin. Initially, a little surprised by my questions about the two boys, Donna quickly understood. This was not the first BCS worker to personally catch the adoption bug.

"However," she said, "you would not be allowed to adopt the six-year-old. Since his mother is your client, it would be considered a conflict of interest."

"Can we get more information on the Romanian child?" I wanted to know, not even sure how to pronounce his name.

Donna gave me the name and contact information of the international adoption worker in Michigan who managed adoptions from Romania.

It would be the first of many calls, and later emails, to Jayne that I would have over the next year and a half.

While we waited eight or nine weeks for information, we had many conversations about our family potentially growing.

"Should we ask our parents what they think?"

"Well, we didn't ask them about having our first two."

"Right."

"But maybe we ought to let those two know what we're thinking."

"That makes sense. After we inform them, we can inform the parents later."

Our son, Aaron, and his fiancé Jenny were house shopping and asked us to come along. From the backseat, I asked Aaron, "Do you remember how you used to always ask for a baby brother?"

"Yeah," he replied as he turned yet another corner.

"Is it too late?"

With shock in his voice, Aaron turned to look at me. "Are you *pregnant*?"

Laughing, Ron and I spilled our plans.

Recovering from the shock, he and Jenny both affirmed that they believed it was not unthinkable and they would support us.

Later, back home, we phoned our daughter Kara in Seattle.

With the two-hour time difference, we often had to leave a message, so I was prepared to say, "Call us when Todd is home too," to the answering machine. To our surprise, Kara answered and had time to talk, which was very uncommon. Confirming that Todd was home, we asked for him to get on the call too. After the usual catch-up chat, I said, "We called to give you some news."

Retelling my dream to them was easy now that I'd told it so many times. Ron also told them that he wanted a letter from God.

"OK," Kara said slowly.

"So we went to church, and Pastor Tim was preaching from Second Samuel, chapter nine."

"About Mephibosheth," said Todd. "We were just talking about that last night."

Oh, come on now! How many people are talking about Mephibosheth? Most people have never heard of him, and few of those who have can say his name. God, you really have a sense of humor!

We discussed it a little more and were surprised to hear our daughter say, "I always knew you would someday adopt."

I will sing of the steadfast love of the Lord,
forever; with my mouth I will make known
your faithfulness to all generations.

Psalm 89:1, ESV

GRANDPARENTS AGAIN

The next time we were in Platteville, where Ron's parents and my mom lived, we made a point of telling them. Ron's mom was pleased, all in favor of the plan, but doubted it would really happen. Ever the one to please, she was encouraging.

His dad and second wife couldn't think of any reason not to go forward but cautioned that it could all go south. Not one of their warnings was anything I hadn't already thought about. Yet I appreciated the candid conversation. Perhaps Ron had not thought about some of them, and I didn't want to be the one bringing up negative possibilities. It gave us much to discuss later, on our way home.

Mom had been forty when I was born, so I didn't expect her response. "Are you nuts? Why would you want to start all over?"

I had a younger brother by two years, along with three older siblings. I reminded Mom, "You were forty-five when dad died, and you raised five of us alone. Don't you believe Ron and I together can raise just one more?"

"It wasn't by choice," she sputtered. "You don't have to do this, but I know you will."

We left, not really feeling victorious but determined to obey God. He would close the doors if it was not meant to be. But we knew He wanted us to be willing.

No one will shut what He opens; no one will open what He shuts.

Isaiah 22:22

HERITAGE

One day, when I was working outside in the yard, a car pulled into the driveway. Out of the car stepped Elmer Dixon, an elderly man of short stature but a large heart. Two decades before, we had purchased this farm from Elmer and his even shorter wife, Nellie. Elmer would often drive by but would only stop if someone were outside. Noticing all the tall elms, he reminisced about planting those years ago, as old folks are wont to do. Then he gestured at the large farmhouse. Knowing our kids had now grown to be adults, he asked about the Dixon House Bed and Breakfast we now ran. Once, he had told me that Nellie always wanted to do that.

Elmer was a bit surprised when I informed him we would not be running the Dixon House very many more months.

"Oh, why is that?"

I told him of our plans to adopt an orphan from Romania. Then it was my turn to be surprised.

"It was 1920 when I was dropped here on this doorstep as a twelve-year-old orphan," he said softly.

He went on to tell me he had been in an orphanage and then selected by Francis and Emma Dixon, who owned this dairy farm. There he grew up and inherited the farm when they passed away. He married Nellie Brown in 1951 when they were both in their forties. Having no children to leave the farm to, they sold it to us in 1980, when they retired and moved into town.

Prior to his death on January 9, 1997, Elmer established funds to provide scholarships to young people pursuing education in protestant Christian ministry or agriculture. He also set up a medical fund to provide medical assistance to children with special needs not covered by insurance.

"The days of the blameless are known to the Lord,
and their inheritance will endure forever."

PSALM 37:18

HIS SUPPLY OF GLORIOUS RICHES

Slowly, more information came from Michigan about this child. Medically, the doctor of the orphanage believed he had no problems. His limb deficiencies were not caused by anything his mother had done during her pregnancy. They had a thorough medical questionnaire completed by his father. "Parents were married and happily expecting their first child. Mother received good prenatal nutrition and care. No alcohol or drugs were used by her during the pregnancy. Both were shocked and grieved by his condition at birth."

Developmentally, he was noted to be obtaining usual pediatric milestones. Baby teeth came in when they should, allowing him to eat and begin forming words. He showed no signs of hearing or vision problems. Sitting up and crawling began when other children his age were doing the same. He was reported to be bright and happy, with a hearty laugh that endeared all his caretakers. When other children began walking, so did Ionut—on his knees.

As we learned more and felt we could deal with the issues, we began the adoption process. Initially, we would have to apply for a home study. Bethany could not do this piece, as I was an employee. We contacted Lutheran Social Services (LSS) and began the paperwork. Now this would not only be an international adoption (complicated in itself) but it would also be an *interagency* adoption. Romanian adoption laws were cumbersome, including the requirement for adoptive parents to travel there for court proceedings to bring their child home.

Lest you think that an employee receives "discounts" on adoption services, let me assure you, that is not the case. Not only would we be expected to pay the typical Bethany fees, but we would also have to pay an application fee and home study fee to LSS. Not inherently wealthy people, we were certainly going to have to be frugal in other areas and trust God to provide the thousands we did not have. My thoughts on the matter:

"Father, you own the cattle on a thousand hills. Are you willing to sell a couple so we can bring him home?"

As I would complete a set of required documents, we would pay the fee for that, then start on the next. We had to provide original birth certificates, passports, marriage certificate, and a host of other documents. Although Ron grew up in southwestern Wisconsin, he was born in Dubuque, Iowa. That meant we had to send fees and apply to that county seat for an original birth certificate. When we received it, we included it in the bundle of papers to be sent to Michigan as our "dossier."

We soon learned that his birth certificate was inadequate. Although it had the county seal of authenticity on it, we needed one from Des Moines, Iowa, bearing the state seal, meaning yet another delay. When all of it was received in Michigan, it was reviewed there before everything was sent on to Washington, DC. There it had a two-week turnaround for review before being sent to Romania.

Once in Bucharest, it needed to be translated before the Romanian Adoption Committee reviewed it and set a court date—at least a month later.

We still owned the land, renting it to another farmer. We also rented the barn to a young fellow getting started with milking his small herd of Holstein cows. That income did not even cover our expenses for the farm. Ron had only been employed for two or three years after selling our cows. He was gaining traction as a salesman in the ag business, and most of our income was from his current employment. Living frugally, we started saving whatever I earned from my small salary at Bethany to offset our adoption expenses.

Funds came from other surprising places, too, as we made progress on the paperwork. Once, when I had been reviewing and totaling the financial worksheet, I became overwhelmed and began discussing it with Ron. Not understanding or accepting the reasons for "ALL THAT MONEY," he had forgotten the Romanian international portion of $6,500 and wondered—with not just a little anger—where would *that* come from? I saw no value in trying to explain or defend the fee. Nor was I about to join in his frustration. We were then interrupted and did not have to continue the conversation. We agreed to discuss it later. The mail arrived before "later" did. Included in the mail was a check for $6,100!

Amazed, I thanked God:

My Father, you ***did*** *sell a cow!* Philippians 4:19 came to mind: "My God will meet all your needs according to the riches of his glory in Christ Jesus."

My younger brother also surprised us with a significant check, as did some of our close friends. We did not have to borrow or do any fundraising.

Preparations also included background checks and a trip to the Immigration and Naturalization Service in Milwaukee for fingerprints, as this was an international adoption. While at the INS Office, we waited with an elderly couple, Olga and Henri, who were there to finalize their citizenship. Although they'd lived in the US for almost forty years, they recently decided to become citizens. When they inquired about our reason for being there, we had the opportunity to share our story of my dream and plans to adopt. They were deeply moved that God would speak so personally to anyone.

We enjoyed the creative activity of preparing a little booklet of pictures of ourselves, our family, and our home. This was then sent to Romania, where Gabi, our Romanian social worker, would take it to show Ionut his new family. Searching scrapbooks, I selected those that included not only us but grandparents, our adult children, and the farm where we lived. This was embellished with captions and stickers before sending it off to the orphanage to show Ionut so he would get to "know" us.

Early in the process of preparing our dossier, we explored the matter of health insurance for Ionut. Calling the human resources (HR) department of his employer, Ron inquired about coverage of prosthetics.

After exploring all the fine print, the HR director assured him that once a child was adopted and legally ours, he was considered the same as one born to us. No insurance benefits could be withheld based on adoption. "Prosthetics and durable medical equipment" were covered with the same deductibles and co-pays of other medical care. Knowing this was a great relief, so we pressed into the paperwork process.

Be still before the Lord and wait patiently for him;
do not fret when people succeed in their ways.

Psalm 37:7

MEALS, MEALS, AND MESSES

With the paperwork all approved and submitted, we waited. Friends and family often asked if we were ready—ready for the arrival of Ionut. Were we ready to give up our freedom, to have mounds of laundry, toys, and meals, more meals, and messes? Was I ready to give up my time alone and exchange my tidy, clean home and routine for chaos and disorder? Those questions came from the understanding ones.

Others told us bluntly that we were crazy, asking for trouble, and on and on. They would continue with their protests, pointing out the trials and sorrows ahead, pointing out our "foolishness" as though we surely had not thought this through. Determined to discourage us, they never stopped with their doubts and questions. "What about college expenses?" College? Are you kidding? This is not about college; this is about obedience to God and becoming a family for an orphan.

They are most to be pitied and prayed for. By hearing and obeying

His voice, we were a serious threat to those who jealously guarded their own comfort and sense of control. We learned that the law of the world is self-protection, while the law of love is self-sacrifice.

The question of readiness did motivate me, however. Hearing that question often, I tried to address it. I wanted to get a room ready, much as any new mom would for a baby or adopted child. Painting, carpeting, and furnishing a room, as well as shopping for clothing, toys, car seat, and more, provided an outlet for my nervous energy.

Equally important to me, however, was to prepare our hearts. I prayed that our attitudes and resources would be ready. Mary, a teenager, was physically unprepared for Jesus, but he arrived, nevertheless. She simply said, "Here I am; let it be according to your word." And she gave birth and laid Him in a manger because there was no room for Him in the inn.

It is so easy to put too much emphasis on the *place.* I did not want Ionut to feel like he was an afterthought or an ornament in the home of a middle-aged couple. I also did not want him to feel that this home was any better or worse than his current one. So does that room make the home? Or do the parents? We could express our love and anticipation by preparing a place fit for a child, but we also decided to prepare our hearts and resources.

In my Father's house are many rooms. If it were not so, would I have told you that I go to prepare a place for you?

JOHN 14:2, ESV

COMMITMENT TESTED

While my focus was on preparations, Ron's was on the obvious need to provide for an additional family member. Weeks after his assurance that his company would include Ionut in the family health insurance, Ron was called into the office by the company owners. They "highly recommended" that he purchase private health insurance so he would not burden the other employees with insurance claims to the collective pool. They would not be able to promise his retention if a "reduction in sales occurred" following claims to the health insurance. Stunned, he excused himself from the meeting to drive home. On the long drive home, he pondered how to process this clearly illegal threat. Like Joseph, Jesus' adoptive father, he was feeling the ridicule of others along with the burden of responsibility.

Not sure what else to do, he was on the road again working the very next day. At one point, he noticed this advertisement painted on the side of a semitruck as it turned: Shriner's Hospital for Children

1-800-237-5055. The artwork featured children with crutches and wheelchairs. The message was a clear answer to prayer.

Being sure to get our attention, I saw a similar truck with the same graphic that very same day. Talking about it later, we understood that we were to apply for his care through a children's hospital that would not only provide care without billing us or the insurance company, but it would also be the best available care.

Ron contacted his employer to assure them that he would not be making claims any more significant than he was entitled to. We also contacted a local prosthetist, Marty Ryan, who assured us that he would service the smaller issues without billing us. He was very helpful in providing information and professional care for many years to come. He continues to be Ionut's "go-to leg man."

Commit your way to the Lord; trust
in Him also and He will do it.

PSALM 37:5, AMP

SHOWERED WITH BLESSING

Romanian orphans have no belongings of their own. Donated clothing, most often used, is stacked according to size. Underpaid nannies dress the babies and children in whatever size fits them, with no regard to styles or patterns appropriate to gender. Children are fed the best they can be with whatever is available. We'd read disturbing articles and anecdotes of children being quite malnourished and small for their age.

Communism had left a tradition of bribery throughout the culture. Some orphanage directors were still in the habit of accepting bribes for better or quicker services to adoptive parents. Bethany, a Christian adoption agency, strictly forbids that practice. If even one family offered what they only considered a small tip above the required fees, others would be expected to, and it would never stop, further corrupting the system.

These two opposing facts left us with a dilemma. How could we adopt only one child, remove him from poverty, and not help the ones who remained in his orphanage? We would not contribute to a bribery system even if we had the resources to do so, which we did not. All fees would be paid in advance to the agency, who would transfer appropriately to the agency in Romania. No cash or monetary exchange while we were there would be allowed.

Trust in the Lord in all of your ways and lean not on your own understanding.

PROVERBS 3:5

Asking for advice from our agency, they suggested we could bring toys or articles of clothing to donate to the orphanage. When I discussed this with a friend, she took that idea and planned a shower for September 22, 1998. Treating us like a family anticipating the birth of a first baby, the whole church was invited to hear our story and bring a gift for the orphanage. Entire families came, bringing an abundance of supplies and gifts. Many also brought clothing for Ionut, knowing we would also need to outfit him and provide toys and more. My favorite articles for him soon became the little overalls because he could crawl without crawling out of them. Without feet to prevent their creeping down, the overall straps held them on his little frame as he moved around. I soon learned that sewing old shoulder pads into the knees and then sewing the legs closed would also be helpful.

Many who had been touched by adoption themselves but didn't know us personally showed up to encourage us and bless us. After hearing our story of a dream, a letter, and obedience, they shared their stories. Others were inspired to investigate adoption or become foster parents themselves. We were overwhelmed with gratitude for all these people who wanted to bless not only us but also little children they would never meet.

The Lord watches over the foreigner
and sustains the fatherless.

Psalm 146:9

ARRIVAL IN BUCHAREST

On November 30, 1998, I wrote in my journal: "Two weeks after our son's wedding and one day after my forty-eighth birthday, we depart for Romania. We leave our comfortable empty nest, going to places we have never been, to return in two weeks with a toddler we've yet to meet. Like a squirrel leaping from one tree to the next, missing the branch she intended but landing on another, we may have a destination or future in view, but until we take the risk of leaving, we can be sure we will never arrive. Even if we miss the one we are aiming for—and life on the other side is much different than we now expect—we know that God can be trusted to take us exactly where He plans for us to go.

"Though many will not understand, some even believing we are crazy, we are excited and thrilled to finally be going to our son to claim and adopt him for our own. In my spirit, I heard Jesus say: 'Although some would think I AM crazy to want to adopt a sinner like you with all your baggage, I left heaven to do it.'"

Ann Haugen picked us up at 11:30 a.m. to drive us to Chicago O'Hare Airport, although we were anxiously prepared to leave hours earlier. We did not want to arrive too early and just sit around at the airport, however. Ann's calm support and prayers were just what we needed to calm our jitters.

Our flight to Zurich, Switzerland, was a long, uneventful seven hours, very much like a domestic flight in every other way. With a seven-hour time change, we arrived in Zurich at 8:20 a.m. on December 1. The airport was very modern and clean, with typical European shops and restaurants bustling in business. After a much-needed cup of strong Swiss coffee, we waited at the departure gate for Bucharest. Of course, now it was beginning to seem very much more international. Travelers and businessmen were going to Geneva, Lagos, Nigeria, and Israel. Fewer and fewer people were speaking English.

We had been advised to fly TAROM Airlines so that flight attendants could help us translate our son's needs on the return flight. After three long hours, along with many Romanians, we boarded the plane for Bucharest. Before we even took off, I closed my eyes and fell asleep. A flight attendant soon woke me up to offer a meal. I accepted it but ate only a few bites before falling asleep again. The next thing I knew, the captain was announcing our descent to Bucharest. I was so tired that the excitement had vanished, and it all felt like a dream.

Once inside the Henri Coandă International Airport in Otopeni, we walked through a very long, hot hallway into an area where everyone waited in lines to have passports checked. The huge room was dimly lit by a single light bulb high in the ceiling. The walls and floor were bare concrete, with not a chair or bench in sight for travelers—very, very different from the modern airport in Zurich. Ron, dressed in khakis and a green coat, and I in jeans with a red coat, were quite obviously Americans, especially when we spoke to each other. Everyone around us was wearing shades of gray and black. A friendly man behind us looked Romanian but wore a red jacket and occasionally remarked in English.

After passing through customs and collecting our luggage, we were met by Dragos, holding a sign reading: "IONUT." Bethany had arranged for this nice young English-speaking fellow to meet us and drive us to the apartment, where we would rest a while before taking the train to Iasi. He not only explained things to us but was also helpful in dealing with the cadre of young boys expecting us Americans to tip them for carrying our luggage. Dragos explained that if we allowed them to help us, they would steal from us when we opened a wallet to hand them a few dollars.

Along the way, we saw downtown, the Russian Embassy, the Arch de Triumph, as well as various banks and government buildings. Who could miss the massive stone building covering several blocks built by Ceauşescu to exalt himself? Dragos and the locals were disgusted by its presence, mocking their poverty while flaunting opulence and grandiose size.

Our hosts, Janet and Florin, lived about a block away in a lovely, spacious apartment. Janet was a beautiful, friendly middle-aged nurse who spoke no English. Florin, a radiologist, also spoke only Romanian. We were assured, though, that their son Allen—a doctor fluent in English—would soon be home. Shortly after Allen arrived, we had dinner together. The table was elegantly set, and the meal was roasted chicken, fried potatoes, pickled red peppers, bread, and a divine dessert—custard pudding with caramel sauce.

But Janet was the best! She was a very gracious hostess and delighted that I was also a nurse. They had been briefed about the child we were adopting, and Bethany chose them to be our hosts as we arrived and then departed later with our child. Janet worked in physical therapy, and Allen's specialty was rehab. They were delighted with Ionut's pictures, and she gave me a big hug to show me she was pleased with us. Love does not require the same language. This greatly eased Ron's mind that we would be with a doctor and a nurse when we returned to Bucharest and then left for home.

Jacob also went on his way, and the angels of God met him.

GENESIS 32:1

TRAIN TO IASI

After resting on December 1, 1998, Janet woke us up to give us some more pudding. Then we went by taxi to the train. Allen was kind enough to go with us to direct us onto the right train and into our sleeping compartment. We had been advised to take a night train so we could lie down and sleep the six hours it would take to get to Iasi.

The Christmas lights of the city were beautiful, and the falling snow made me think of the movie *Dr. Zhivago*. This train ride was like stepping back in time at least four decades. We had been cautioned to dress warmly: "There won't be much heat on the train—if any." It did not take Ron very long to fall asleep on the lower berth. My walk to the bathroom was the next indicator of the past. There was no plumbing in sight, and a hole in the floor to the tracks below was considered a toilet.

Really? While this train is rocking back and forth?

While I did have tissues in my pocket, this was before the days of hand sanitizers.

Back in our compartment, I climbed into the top berth and, using a flashlight, began to journal. First, I shed the coat, then a sweater, and it was still hot inside the cramped compartment. Noticing my inaudible complaining, I heard the still small voice:

I left paradise, or heaven, coming to this fallen world for thirty-three years to rescue you and all sinners. I am only asking you to leave your comforts for two weeks to rescue one child.

That was all I needed to end my attitude of complaining during the entire trip.

As our journey continued, sleep eluded me while Ron slept soundly below. The gentle purring and occasional snore verified his slumber. Around five in the morning, I got so worried when we sat, not moving, that I woke him up. I was afraid we had missed our stop and were returning to Bucharest when the train finally began to roll again. It seemed to go in the direction we had come. So he went to ask a porter, who just laughed, assuring us he would let us know when we were almost to Iasi.

Apparently, it was one of those stations where the tracks form a Y, and we had stopped in the stem. The caboose was replaced by an engine that was now pulling the other end of the train off again to the north. A little over an hour later, the porter came to our compartment to announce our pending arrival.

Just as planned, our social worker Gabi was on the platform when our train arrived in Iasi at six-thirty. Her husband, Daniel, drove us in his old Dacia to their apartment for a nap and some breakfast. Anxious to go to the orphanage but also exhausted and hungry, we welcomed the reprieve.

But when the fullness of the time came, God sent His Son, born of a woman, born under the Law, so that He might redeem those who were under the Law, that we might receive the adoption as sons and daughters.

Galatians 4:4–5, NASB

IASI AT LAST

Wednesday, December 2, 1998

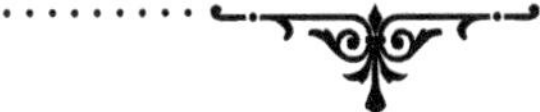

It was bitterly cold that week in December. Gabi and Daniel lived in a one-bedroom apartment in one of the concrete structures built during communism. It was not near a city heating plant, so it was cold all the time. They explained to us later that heat was produced by massive boilers housed in central locations. The heated air was blown through enormous pipes to other buildings several blocks away. *This explains why it was so hot at Janet and Florin's, even with windows often open. They lived right next to the heating plant.*

We were given the best of hospitality. Daniel and Gabi slept on a futon in the main room so that we could have the bed and privacy of their bedroom. Meals were eaten in the small, combined living room/dining room. I was not permitted to help with anything in the kitchen because it was literally big enough for only one person at a time.

There had been a lot of snow, and it was piled in dirty mounds everywhere. Streets were covered with roughly packed dirty snow—not plowed or cleaned to the standards we expect in America. In this large city, people walked, which they found to be less difficult than driving cars in those conditions.

Late morning, we were taken to St. Parascheva's Orphanage to finally meet Ionut. Unlike the horrible institutions we had seen on the *60 Minutes* exposé, this was a large, clean, well-maintained, and brightly lit classical building. Gabi later explained that most are like what we had seen on TV. This one, however, was the one the government allowed Americans into. Instead of going right to the area where Ionut would be, they led us to a large meeting room where the director, another social worker, the doctor, and other adults were seated. Soon, one of the caretakers carried in a little blonde child and introduced us.

Ionut was every bit as cute as his photos depicted him. He was even cuter in person, with an incredibly happy face that easily broke into giggles. I was smitten, loving him instantly as tears of joy filled my heart and eyes. He seemed to recognize that we were the people in the photos that were sent to the orphanage for him. He was naturally a little shy, and because the staffers could speak to him in his own tongue, and they all spoke to him at once, he was paying more attention to them. After a little playing around, giggles, and laughs, we were escorted out. The visit was brief, and we were assured by Gabi that we would return later the same day.

Whatever happens, conduct yourselves in a manner worthy of the gospel of Christ.

PHILIPPIANS 1:27

GOOD NIGHT MOON

Having some experience with adoption, there was one thing about which I was especially concerned. Due to a lack of nurturing and pleasant attention, many orphans have a tough time trusting adults. They receive so little response to their needs that they develop ways to comfort themselves or just hide within themselves. Often, orphans are overly and falsely affectionate towards adults, manipulating them to get their needs met while withholding genuine trust. Others remain obviously detached and unable to emotionally connect with anyone. Those who receive the least attention seem to be at the greatest risk for radical attachment disorder, preventing their ability to bond with new parents.

What would it be like for Ionut? Would he trust us? Would there be extremely difficult behavior?

After another nap and more of Gabi's delicious food, Daniel drove us all back for a late afternoon visit. This time we went into the room where he and dozens of other toddlers were seated around little tables for their supper. I was encouraged to feed him—a mixture of scrambled eggs and mamaliga (polenta). *He is almost four; why isn't he feeding himself? And why is he in this group of children that appear to be one and a half to two years old?*

When he was finished eating, he showed us the room where all the boys slept. Rows of small white cribs with clean linens lined the room. Nice nursery curtains draped the windows. Two or three little boys were sitting on potty chairs (each crib had one beside it), and others were playing. Ron and Ionut were tossing a little toy we brought back and forth when suddenly the lights went out.

Because of his fear of the dark, Ionut was screaming and clinging to me, so I just held and comforted him. Fortunately, all the caretakers were rushing to find candles and trying to quiet all the other screaming little ones, so no one rushed to grab him from my arms. I walked calmly to a window, where the full moon shone in, and sang silly soothing songs to him.

By the time the lights came back on, Ron had two or three little girls hanging on him. A little Maria especially endeared him. Before our trip, I had prepared myself to focus only on our child, so my heart would not break at leaving other children there. Silently I thanked God for His unique way of providing those bonding moments.

Gabi later explained to me that Ionut's handicaps were one of God's ways to ensure his ability to bond. Lacking feet, he had to be carried like a baby, much longer than the other children. She also explained that babies with handicaps have either one effect or another on the caretakers. Some adults are superstitious and avoid the little ones with differences. In his case, they found him sweet and endearing, so he was quite spoiled.

Thank you, dear Father. I would rather have him spoiled and able to bond than have him detached and unemotional.

When the lights returned, I assumed his care. After some fun and silly games, we got him ready for bed. It was a precious time of bonding for the three of us as he giggled and retrieved the little soft toys we threw about. Soon, though, we were ushered out. Sadly, we had to leave Ionut there while we completed legal work over the next few days under Gabi's guidance.

Whether it was jet lag and time zone adjustment or so much excitement, sleep again eluded me once back at Gabi's apartment. I needed to process all that had happened. When you meet your child for the first time, and that child is nearly four years old, you wonder what he has been through. You wonder how he was cared for. You wonder if he will be happy to leave or will want to stay where he is familiar with everyone. You also wonder how you will ever accomplish all the legal paperwork that must be completed before you can all board a flight to return to Wisconsin.

When I look at the sky and see the work of your fingers—the moon and the stars you set in place—what are mere mortals that you should think about them, human beings that you should care for them?

PSALM 8:3–4

GOTCHA DAY

Gabi had scheduled our final court appearance for December 4, 1998. We had paperwork and documents to complete, copy, and translate before the appearance. Starting early in the morning, she directed us to the appropriate office to complete the next step. The air was bitterly cold—"frig," as the locals spoke—and the streets were sloppy and slushy. Snow removal was not a priority for the city, so drivers were obliged to do the best they could, slipping, sliding, and spinning through the packed snow and ice that accumulated with months of dirt and grime. I soon understood why Romanians wore only dark clothing and dressed in three or four layers. Errands were more easily accomplished on foot than by vehicle.

We needed to go to government buildings to sign decrees and change the birth certificate. The official birth certificate would declare us as his mother and father. We learned later that it was a "certificate of birth facts." *Strange*, I thought. How does rewording and changing names on a paper change the facts of birth?

Each official document had to be taken to a typist and typed with multiple copies made of each. Bethany did not have their own office, so this paperwork was all taken to a tiny office that existed only for the purpose of typing and making copies. It was a tiny little storefront with a drafty door and windows. The two typists worked at manual Smith Corona typewriters that were decades old. The ancient Xerox machines were babied along to function for another decade or two. We would drop off the papers, with Gabi explaining to the ladies wearing coats and gloves in their unheated space about what was needed, then returning later to pick them up.

In the meantime, we explored some aged, very historic buildings such as the courthouse, opera house, and orthodox cathedral. Gabi took us inside St. Parascheva's Cathedral. A line of people stood along one side of the room that was partially enclosed. One by one, a priest allowed them to go inside. Asking about this unusual sight in the middle of the week, Gabi explained. "They are very superstitious. They believe that St. Parascheva's mummy is in there, and if they touch it, they will have good luck or healing for a family member." The place had a musty smell of incense and a creepy feel to it. I was happy to exit back out into the fresh air, praying that God would reveal himself and the truth to those people.

We returned to pick up all our documents, then moved on to the courthouse. We were called into a beautiful courtroom along with Gabi, who presented the lovely lady judge wearing a fur hat and coat with our paperwork. After reading these, she looked at us and thanked us for our commitment to adopting this little boy and gave us her blessing along with the official stamp on the necessary documents.

Daniel returned us to the orphanage, where we met the director with papers in hand. We also delivered the extra children's clothes and toys we had brought with us. She then escorted us to where

Ionut was waiting. I had been instructed to bring along a sedative to help him relax for the new and frightening adventure. After giving it to him, we dressed him in the garments we brought for him. We played with him for about thirty minutes and were then told to go. They all wanted hugs and sweet goodbyes, but sensing it was final, he began to wail loudly, and we were hurried out the door, carrying our screeching, panicking child.

Daniel's vehicle, like most others, was an old Dacia manufactured locally. The heater did not work very well, but the radio and tape player functioned well. We were thankful for that, as the only thing that calmed our frightened little boy was loudly playing Daniel's cassette tape of *ABBA Gold*. Having never been out of the orphanage, Ionut was terrified of traveling in a vehicle with his new adult companions. Child car seats were not required, so they were also unavailable. Holding him on my lap while in the car was our only option. We all sang along with ABBA, and he soon joined in the *musica*.

Arriving back at Gabi and Daniel's apartment, she gave our little boy a tour along with instructions to be a good boy. She explained to him that he would sleep with us there for a few nights, then travel with us to America to begin his life in a forever family. His curiosity and enthusiasm energized all of us after our extremely long day.

Gabi served us dinner at the table while she and Daniel sat on the couch to eat. She always had tasty meals to warm up for us. Her mother had come prior to our visit to cook many meals and freeze them. Although I offered to help with dishes, she insisted I just spend time with Ionut. Again, her kitchen had room for only one person anyway.

The first night was restless and sleepless for us. Exhausted, Ionut fell asleep without a struggle but awoke after only a couple of hours sobbing and rocking himself. Probably homesick, he was inconsolable. We let him play with the flashlight for a while, and he slept another hour or two. Awake again, in need of a bath and change of clothes, we gave up expecting him to sleep.

God sets the lonely in families.

PSALM 68:6

SIGHTSEEING

Others in the adoption loop advised us to spend time exploring the city where our child was born. You never know if you will ever return. Should this be your only visit, it's best to find out what you can about the area and culture. Years later, when your child asks questions, you will be able to provide descriptions and context to his origins. It will also help you understand his roots a little better.

With Gabi and Daniel as tour guides, we heeded that advice. We shopped in the small markets for daily needs, such as long underwear for Ron, who was always cold, but especially outside. We also picked up diapers. Ionut was not potty trained as we had been told. Or the sudden changes were so severe that he relapsed into a previous state of development.

Souvenir shopping was remarkably interesting. The beautiful lace, embroidery, and pottery displayed local artistry. Downtown Iasi had been a beautiful city prior to communism and was making a comeback. Staircases and columns of marble were more common than concrete sidewalks. The architecture of the opera house, courthouse, library, cathedrals, and other buildings was very classical and "Old World." We saw the hospital where Ionut was born from only the outside. He was in wonder at all the sights, sounds, and tastes. The inside of the orphanage was all he knew.

A central park with a statue of St. George provided a good outdoor stroll for families and young lovers. Someone had made a snowman, which was a very amusing sight for Ionut. We used an umbrella stroller to transport Ionut about, as he would become too heavy for us to carry. With a coat on and a blanket around him, the stares and scolding of others were limited to those who did not think a child should be outside in the cold.

Nearby was a lovely arboretum where we escaped the cold to enjoy rows of beautiful plants inside warm greenhouses. Ionut was delighted to toss coins into the goldfish pond. We enjoyed an elegant dessert together before venturing back out into the cold.

Eventually, I needed a restroom. Gabi was very reluctant to allow me to use any. She walked us three blocks to a hospital, and we went inside. Thinking we would find one for visitors on the first floor, she instead ushered me up a concrete stairway. A doctor attempted to stop us, but in Romanian, she explained that we were Americans and needed *clean* restrooms. Ushering me inside one, a doctor emerged, wiping her wet hands on her lab coat. There were no doors on the stalls and no soap at the sinks. Although there were no paper towels or hand dryers, there was toilet paper. Later, Gabi explained that at least those bathrooms had flush toilets. I thought to myself, *If these are the best ones she could find for us, I really did not want to see the ones we avoided.*

We then stopped at a café for pizza and beers, having a good laugh about it and trying to remember the highlights of the day. Riding in Daniel's Dacia had become an adventure Ionut enjoyed, singing along to Celine Dion and *ABBA Gold*. Back at their apartment, we listened to Romanian Christmas *musica*.

As I fell asleep, I was thinking about it being the second Sunday of Advent. We would be entering another Christmas season with a child, I realized. That night, we all slept a little better.

And Mary said: "My soul glorifies the Lord."

Luke 1:46

BACK TO BUCHAREST

We were out of bed before 4:30 a.m. and into Daniel's car (*la mașină*) by 5:15 a.m., making our way through the filthy gray snow to the train. Sadly, it was time to say goodbye to Gabi and Daniel, who had done so much for us.

Departing promptly at 6:00 a.m., this was a modern train, not at all like the one we used to travel into Iasi on the night of December 1. We occupied a clean compartment of six seats—for just the three of us and one Romanian businessman. Although it was a long six-hour ride, we were comfortable, and Gabi had sent sandwiches and bottled water for us to "keep up our strength." Ionut would not allow us to remove his coat and hat or even be off my lap long enough for me to remove mine. The train car was so warm I began to wonder if I would pass out from the heat. Ionut would not even allow a *mănușă* (mitten) to be removed.

Mickey, the social worker from Bethany, was on the platform, right at the door, to meet us as we stepped off the train in Bucharest. She and Florin helped us with luggage to Florin's car, then drove us to Janet and Alexander's apartment. I was so tired and overheated that I could hardly think. But they pointed out the palace of Ceaușescu, the now-executed dictator, as we passed. Completely occupying a few city blocks, the palace was visible across the street from Janet's apartment. There, Mickey wanted to review paperwork, so Daddy (Tata) did that while I finally removed my coat and lay down.

After a nap, we had a delicious dinner prepared by Florin. *Are all Romanians such good cooks*? I wondered. Who knew that soup, potatoes, and pork chops could taste and smell this wonderful? Janet and Florin's apartment was close to the heat center, so often, their windows were open to let out the excess heat. Their home was very spacious and elegant—furnished with beautiful carved cabinetry and furniture, lush with many green plants and fresh yellow roses adorning the tables, and elegant linens and china in everyday use.

With renewed energy, Ionut was active and, of course, the center of attention. He explored new things. *Lumina* (light) on, *lumina* off. He adored their cat, Bootsu, which is Romanian for kitty. He chased the cat around on his hands and knees, giggling and trying to get the cat to chase the *mașina* (Hot Wheels car), which Bootsu merrily obliged. Although we spoke no Romanian, and they no English, it did not matter, for laughter is universal. Many years later, in Wisconsin, we would name a kitten Bootsu and recall these happy times.

Janet dialed the phone to call her son, Allen, who spoke English. Putting the phone to Ionut's ear, he became confused. He was looking for Allen, whose voice he could hear but whose face he couldn't see. This being his first experience with a phone, he called it *allo* as everyone seemed to begin saying "allo" to it or from it.

There is a time for everything, and a season for every activity under the heavens.

ECCLESIASTES 3:1

FEARFULLY AND WONDERFULLY MADE

After a good breakfast prepared by Allen, we were transported by Florin in his little white Dacia to Ionut's medical exam. Adopted children must be cleared of any communicable diseases before entering the United States.

The first room we went to was reasonably clean but sparsely appointed for a doctor's office. Primitively furnished, it sported a bare table, a few chairs, and a small space heater. Someone declared this to be the wrong location, and we were then escorted to a nearby hospital.

Upon entering an exam room, we noted the cot with fresh linens, assorted toys, and many medical supplies. Confirming this to be the right place, a blonde female physician and two nurses arrived to examine Ionut. The doctor was so patient and connected easily with Ionut, winning his and our confidence. She not only reviewed the recent medical report sent along by the orphanage physician, but she also gave him a thorough physical exam, noting and remarking on his good health and pleasant cooperation. Later, I asked Gabi to track down his full medical record and have it translated for his pediatrician back in Wisconsin.

The doctors gave Ionut the green light with a complete record of up-to-date immunizations and no diseases, communicable or otherwise. She also assured us that his limb differences were not the result of any known disease or maternal deficiency and would not lead to any non-orthopedic issues. His internal organs and all systems were within normal limits, as was his cognitive ability. Relieved to have one more requirement completed, we were closer to returning home. We took a break at Janet's apartment, where Allen made us a fine lunch.

Once again, we saw Dragos, our driver from the first night in Bucharest. He now drove us to the American embassy to get approval for Ionut's emigration to the US. This was an elegant Old World style building with carved dark mahogany woodwork. There we met a few other American families in the same process of adoption: Doris and Gary of Sheboygan, Wisconsin, adopting Pavel (Paul); Kathy and her husband of Brookfield, Wisconsin, adopting Jean; and a couple from Houston, Texas, adopting Anna Maria. The parents were all eager to talk to other Americans about this new adventure we were all on and the upcoming challenges of our growing families. The children, *copii,* were delighted and playful with one another.

With our mission accomplished, Dragos drove us back to Janet's apartment, where we could relax and begin packing for our return trip. Allen and his wife, Joanna, were fascinated and entertained by Ionut's energy. He showed off all his new words and tricks to them while we packed belongings into our oversized suitcases.

For you created my inmost being; you knit
me together in my mother's womb.
I praise you because I am fearfully and wonderfully made.

Psalm 139:13–14

LITTLE BLONDE ANGEL

We awoke at 4:00 a.m. on December 11, 1998. Ionut had slept well and woke up in a pleasant mood. *Buno*! After coffee for us and yogurt for him, we said goodbye to Janet and Alex. Before dawn, Dragos drove us all to Otopeni Airport in Bucharest. I tried to fasten in my mind the vision of Christmas lights along the city streets so I could one day describe them to Ionut. He had come so far in a few short days. One week before, he was terribly frightened of the car, but now he was truly excited to go in it. If only we adults could adjust to change as quickly as children do.

Ensuring we were in the correct line to board the correct flight, Dragos waved goodbye, and we were on our own—or sort of. There were other American parents and young children nearby most of the time. And I have a way of forgetting God's presence. *Where can I go from your Spirit? Where can I flee from your presence?*

As this was 1998, before 9/11, it was not such a big ordeal to board an international flight. We were, however, traveling with a toddler and understood almost no Romanian. Our toddler had never been on a plane. The first time he was outside the orphanage was to ride in a car. That had terrified him. Only a couple of days later, we traveled by train, also upsetting him, so we didn't know what to expect when flying. We were using an umbrella stroller for him as he weighed too much for us to carry him constantly and manage our luggage. Without feet, he couldn't be expected to just stand or walk next to us like most three-year-olds. The stroller had to be left at the gate, even though it was technically his wheelchair.

Finally, we were seated on a TAROM jumbo jet with many Romanians and folks returning to the US. Several passengers near us were also accompanied by little ones. Some were new adoptive families like us. Others were escorts for adoption agencies, traveling with former orphans to be adopted as soon as they arrived in the states. Standing while I could before the anticipated hours buckled in a seat, I started a conversation with the lady in the row behind us. She had two little ones with her, so I asked if she was adopting them.

"No," she said. "I am Lori, and I have a private adoption agency, US Adopt. These two have been matched with parents, and I am their escort."

She then asked what our story was. We told her we were bringing home our son, and she asked what city he was from.

"Iasi."

"Which orphanage?"

"St. Parascheva's."

"I've been there many times," she declared happily. "Did you ever see a little blonde boy walking on his knees? I have been praying for him—he was like an angel."

I invited her to stand so she could gaze into his face. "Was it this one?"

Standing to peer over the seat, she exclaimed with tears running down her cheeks, "It is you!" Then she began to chatter excitedly to him in Romanian, and he was very happily responsive. She kept up until we all were required to fasten our seatbelts for takeoff. If anyone thought him an angel before takeoff, his angelic status soon evaporated.

Ionut busied himself with exploring the many buttons on the armrest to adjust the channels and volume of the inflight radio. He was excited as the plane accelerated for takeoff but began to shriek as the plane rose above the clouds. Now, it is well-known that little ones suffer extreme ear pain as the cabin pressure changes to accommodate altitudes. At the time, we didn't know this, and we were sure that it was his fear of the unknown that had overtaken him. After all, he had reacted the same way in the auto and train. Flight attendants provided beverages, hoping swallowing would help or sucking would soothe him, but he wouldn't have it. I could see the terror in his eyes and simply held him close. It took a long time, but the screaming finally waned a few hours into the nonstop flight to Chicago, and he slept, but only briefly. Although exhausted myself, I could not get comfortable enough to even nap.

I prayed for his future, for ours, that we would somehow be enough for one another, thanking God for choosing us to raise him. I prayed for his birth parents, Carmen and Catalin, that somehow, they would know in their hearts that their little boy was now safe with his forever family, who would get him some "feet" and love him always. I prayed they would know Jesus and that he would, too, so that one day they could be reunited.

Until then, we would love him and try to teach him whatever he needed to know to live in this world. I also prayed for the little girl, somewhere in this world, who would someday become his wife. I thanked the Lord for the precious moments Ionut held my shoes on the ends of his legs, hopping around on the floor. I had been so sad realizing that he wouldn't be able to walk around in my shoes as all toddlers do. Then, much to my surprise, he did it his own way!

For the kingdom of God belongs to those who are like these children. I tell you the truth, anyone who doesn't receive the Kingdom of God like a child will never enter it.

Luke 18:16–17, NLT

O'HARE WELCOME

Our son Aaron and his new bride, Jenny, met us at the airport in Chicago. Our hearts filled with joy and celebration when we saw them just outside the gate. Aaron's big grin and strong embrace were matched by Jenny's teary smiles and hugs. Their excitement revived our energy.

Fastened firmly into a proper car seat, Ionut charmed Jenny on one side of him, I on the other. Aaron drove, stopping at a Cracker Barrel for a meal. By now, our little newcomer was no longer afraid of car travel and continued to jabber all the way home, learning more names and words in English.

Late in the afternoon, as dusk was transitioning to dark evening, we arrived home. Our excitement was mounting to a frenzy as we entered our house to find a "Welcome Home" sign from Kay and our church friends. Gifts, food, and cards filled the dining room table. Astonishing Aaron and Jenny, our little guy came "running" along behind me as I gave him a tour of our house, his new home. To their amazement, he even scrambled up the stairs, following me on his knees to his room. Ron's contented chuckle brought up the rear of the parade. Ionut's delight and exclamations of wonder surpassed the reaction of little orphan Annie when she first entered her home. Ron's humble satisfaction was every bit as good as Daddy Warbucks.

When Ionut saw his room, he was overcome with giggles about the few toys he saw around. When Amelia, our tiger-striped cat, appeared, he squealed with delight and tried to follow her under the bed. The kitty had missed us too but was mystified by this new creature.

We decided to save the gifts for the morning and try to calm and quiet down for bed, as it had already been such a long day. So after Aaron and Jenny said goodbye, Ionut had a little supper. His first bath at home was also his first one without screaming. Victory! He was no longer afraid of the water. Still frightened of being alone, I laid down with him on his bed, where he finally fell asleep.

Jet lag, exhaustion, and excitement combined meant we would all awaken early. Having eaten breakfast, we opened two weeks' worth of mail while Ionut opened the many gifts of toys and clothing. I'm not sure who was most excited—but I might have to guess it was Dad—when he read the approval for health insurance, which included adopted children. Ionut was close, though, when he discovered Father Noah and his ark full of animals while listening to Veggie Tales musica.

While Ron went grocery shopping, I took Ionut outside in the stroller. Bundled in snow pants, coat, and hat, he met neighbors Cathy, Leo, and their dog Daisy. They were so eager to welcome him home they dashed outside when they saw us. We still had not told them about his feet and wondered when and how to do that. That would be a frequent challenge in the coming weeks.

A few days later, I composed a Christmas letter that explained about adopting our new son. It did save us from the questions closer friends and relatives would have. Responding to the questions of strangers would be another matter.

Man looks on the outside appearance,
but the Lord looks on the heart.

1 Samuel 16:7, ESV

YOUR NEW NAME SHALL BE

For months we thought about whether we were going to change his name. Many asked about it.

Many experts in the adoption field do not recommend changing the name of a child beyond infancy. Before a child is even a year old, they respond when their name is spoken, so changing that name would be attempting to change their identity. Ionut was nearly four when we finally met him. Everything familiar to him was about to change. He would be lifted out of a daycare-type environment for the first time and placed in a family. Instead of being constantly surrounded by dozens of other needy little ones and a few overworked young adults, he would now be the only child of two older adults. His two new siblings were already adults and not living with us, so now he would essentially be an only child.

Like any three-year-old, he knew his native tongue and was able to speak it. He was about to leave that place and be transplanted into a new culture, where only English was spoken. "At least allow him to take his name with him," they advised.

Guided by that logic, we tried. Not a common name in America, Ionut was often mispronounced or misspelled. We were informed by the American adoption workers to pronounce his name "like the British Ian, adding 'ut' to make it 'EE-yen-ut,' rhyming with *nut.* They were incorrect. It is pronounced "Yo-NOOTZ" (soft y-o followed by emphasis on NOOTZ). Very common in Romania, it is a form of Ion, which translates to John. Ionut translates to Johnny. Since the meaning of John is "blessing from God," we thought it fitting.

After mentally and audibly calling him "EE-a-nut" for weeks, we quickly learned to say "Yo-Noots,' which rolled comfortably off our tongues by the time we returned to the states. Yet others understandably continued to mispronounce and misspell it. To this day, "officials" think he misspelled his own name and correct it to "Lonut." Nicknaming him Noot while legally keeping Ionut made it easier for everyone.

I began to wish I had searched Scripture better on this decision. When I did, I discovered that God actually changed people's names, usually in adulthood, when He revealed His purpose for their life. Abram became Abraham (Genesis 17:5). Sarai became Sarah (Genesis 17:15). Jacob became Israel (Genesis 32:28). In Revelation, God informs us that everyone who is victorious will be given a new name (2:17).

Noot's life was changing. No longer would he be called an orphan but a son. No longer would he be called lonely or afraid but *adopted* into a loving family (Psalm 68:6). No longer would his self-image include self-rejection from comparing himself to others, but he would be positively affirmed as God's creation with value. No longer would he be in the bondage of an orphanage, depending on sympathy to meet his needs. Now he would have the liberty to learn, explore, and fulfill the potential God had placed in him, becoming interdependent and meeting the needs of others while accepting help when needed. No longer would he view authorities as those to be manipulated by charm to get his needs met, but as people he could trust to be loving even in his childish naughtiness. No longer was his future one of hopelessness and despair but filled with possibilities of productivity and purpose.

All of this and much more deserved a new name, which he received after all.

You shall be called by a new name that
the mouth of the Lord will give.

Isaiah 62:2, ESV

DAY BY DAY, WEEK BY WEEK

The next several months were a blur of activity. Trying to establish a routine and rhythm of life was not going to happen quickly. Whatever he may have lacked in body parts, Noot was definitely not lacking in energy or brilliance. Very quickly, he picked up our language as we constantly named everyone and everything.

His constant activity and chattering seemed to be his efforts to make up for lost time. He could easily walk on his knees, so I padded the knees of his pants as our flooring was hardwood, not carpet. When he wanted to go faster, he crawled. Realizing he'd unknowingly crawl out of his pants, I dressed him in bib overalls so the straps over his shoulders would keep them on his little frame. I soon learned that he was easier to pick up off the floor, using those straps as a handle.

Before the end of the month, friends held a "blessing party" for him for his fourth birthday. As he opened all his gifts, each lady put their hand on him, praying a blessing. Now those items are long outgrown and long gone, but the blessings continue.

Believing that Ionut is a gift from the Lord, we dedicated him in February 1999. For his dedication, Pastor Tim selected the verse, "Don't be afraid! I've asked you to come so that I can be kind to you" (2 Samuel 9:7, TLB).

Many of the nights in the early months were interrupted by shrill crying that would not stop. Thinking that grief and confusion were the sources of his night crying, I did my best to comfort him back to sleep. On far too many nights, nothing would console him. Taking him to the dentist revealed that he had cavities in nearly all his teeth. Because there were so many, it was decided to make the necessary repairs under general anesthesia. When the nighttime crying ceased after the dental repairs, we agreed with the dentist. The source of his headaches was likely multiple toothaches.

Bonding continued to increase as well as his language. We enrolled Noot in early childhood classes for two or three purposes. A few hours a couple of mornings a week would help him catch up on the language and personal skills to prepare him for eventual school. I probably don't need to remind you that as a forty-eight-year-old mom, I didn't mind the break either.

A few months later, in September, he would attend James Otis School for 4K. Ironically, that was the school where I had picked up the poster of the poem, "Heaven's Very Special Child." The little school not far from us had only two classrooms. One was for 4K. The other was for a small number of children with autism. At various times, Mrs. Basemen and the other teacher would mix the kids as a life lesson in accepting and participating with those who may be different from themselves. I decided to return the poster to be displayed for all parents.

People began noticing his differences and asking curious questions, and sometimes strangers would ask rudely, "What happened to his feet?" When I had the time, rather than ignore their comments,

I used them as teaching moments. Not wanting Noot to feel like he was different or in any way inferior, I also wanted to inform the questioner. I learned to respond to that question with, "Nothing happened; it's the way God made him. Just as he made some with blue eyes, some with brown."

Often, they noticed his hands before commenting about his lack of feet. Noot has a right hand with fingers that do not bend enough to make a fist, while his left hand is one large digit that he uses like a thumb. Kids, being curious, might ask, "Why does he only have one hand?" I would respond, "Because God made him so smart, he only needs one." As he got older, I would say, "Ask him; he's right here." When kids would stare, he would say politely, "You're probably wondering about . . ." and start a conversation with them.

Do not consider his appearance or his height . . . The Lord does not look at the things people look at. People look at the outward appearance, but the Lord looks at the heart.

1 Samuel 16:7

I GOT SHOES

Many people asked us if we were going to get Ionut fitted for prosthetics. Wanting to give our son time to bond, learn the language, and trust us, we were not in a hurry to start that process. We had done our research and knew there would be many trips to Shriner's Hospital in Chicago and much therapy required for him to adapt to them. We just did not see it as a priority—YET!

In mid-April, we were excited for a long-awaited date night dinner and movie, and a neighborhood teen Alyssa was coming to babysit. While Ron was in the shower getting ready, Ionut wanted to sit on my lap. As I sat down on the couch with him on my lap, I started flipping through TV channels. I landed on a program about a man with a right-below-knee amputation being fitted for a prosthesis. Showing Noot that the man's stump was just like his, we watched as he was measured, fitted, tried on the leg, stood on the leg, and eventually began to run. Using words and hand signals, I told him that one day we would take him to the doctor to get one of those and a foot for his other leg too. His left leg ends at the ankle, his right just above the knee. He had developed quite severe tightness in the left leg by walking so much on his knees, with the rest of his left leg behind him always bent. So I warned him that he would have to exercise that knee to make it straighter.

He did not care! He was so excited and began rapidly and repeatedly bending his leg back and forth, yelling: "Ionut go doctor! Go shopping! Get feet! Get shoes! Run outside! 'Nother one too!" over and over.

In the morning, he had not forgotten. His excited chant continued all the way to church.

Knowing he would expect it to happen very quickly, I devised a way to help him wait. I found a sticker of a prosthetic leg and placed it on the calendar for the day of his first appointment on May 28. Then, of course, we marked off each day until that day arrived. In the meantime, he would repeat his chant to everyone he saw.

Finally, the day came when we would arrive at Shriner's Hospital for Children in Oak Park, Illinois. The waiting room was completely occupied with parents and children with a variety of limb differences and special needs. For once, Ionut was not the object of curious stares. Coming from all over the Midwest, some carried luggage, expecting to stay overnight when surgery would be required.

Dr. Ackman, the orthopedic specialist, was calm and assuring, putting us all at ease. Professionals and students of all things pediatric examined our son while he, in turn, charmed them. When they determined a plan, we were directed to Scheck & Siress Orthotics and Prosthetics, about a mile away. Having been warned that it would take most of the afternoon, we stopped for lunch at Charlie Robinson's Best Ribs. That stop proved to be a tasty way to satisfy not only our waning energy but also our palates.

Check-in at Scheck and Siress was quick and efficient. Friday afternoons were obviously set aside for the children being sent over from Shriners, as several of the same littles were here as well. John Angelico and his assistants cast Ionut's legs for the molds that would be used to make sockets for his "Shriner feet." They asked us how we came to adopt this child from Romania, so we shared how God had led us to him through a dream and a letter. Noot became used to us retelling the story, so at times he would even want to be told again.

Because time would be required to make his prosthetics, they instructed him about exercising his left leg in the meantime in order to relieve the tightness of his knee. The physical therapist also gave him a knee immobilizer to wear at night that would hold it in a straighter position. John also created and completed stiff rubber protectors for his stumps so he could move around freely outdoors on the ground without developing sores or blisters.

Two weeks later, we returned to Oak Park for the first fitting of his new legs and feet. Ron could not take off more work, so my sister Emma accompanied us. Having a second adult not only provided a navigator and company but was also essential for occupying and assisting with Noot's multiple needs. Imagine stopping for gas and food while carrying a twenty-pound baby that you cannot set down on the restroom floor while you use the facilities. Before the days of GPS, taking the right exit and navigating traffic in an unfamiliar city with a chattering toddler was also a challenge that required two sets of adult eyes and ears.

Noot was delighted and animated when he first saw the fabricated legs, trying them on with the help of two prosthetists named John and Walter. We had been told what size shoes to buy, so he picked out a pair of athletic shoes that light up when stepping. They made several adjustments as the prosthetics were refitted and then tweaked again. With their help, he stood tall, looking like the cat that had just swallowed the canary. Holding on to the hand railings for support and balance, he would kick one leg in front of him, then the other, as far out as they would go. We were confident that he would quickly adapt, learning to run and play.

For many days, I could not get this song out of my head: "I got shoes, you got shoes, all God's children got shoes . . ."

A couple of years later, we were talking about heaven when Noot's black-brown eyes looked at me and announced, "I can see piles of fake arms and legs there, as people won't need them when we get our new bodies."

IONUT, AGE SIX

WHEN YOU WALK

The months remaining in 1999 became the months of therapy. There was speech therapy, helping us teach Noot a new language. There was occupational therapy, equipping him to manage life with only one hand and some very stiff fingers. Most often, a physical therapist (PT) would teach him to walk and move about on these "stilts" known as prosthetics. He started PT at Shriner's in Oak Park as an outpatient. I booked a room at the Write Inn, about a mile away, also on Oak Park Avenue, so we could stay nearby. His sessions were morning and afternoon, with a break in between for lunch and a nap back at the hotel.

His PT, Mary, was patient and supportive, teaching him to first don and doff his new legs, then stand and take steps. She had worked with many children and kept a harness around him so she could prevent falls if he lost his balance. She would assist him in walking through the halls, help him climb the play equipment outside, and practice going up and down a long stairway open to the play area. Ionut made friends with all the staff and other children—there was not a shy bone in his body! As the days went by, we could all see he wasn't really relying on the harness or Mary's support. But he was not as confident about walking as he was about making friends.

The Write Inn was the right place to stay. Old but well maintained, it had more character and friendlier staff than the large modern hotels farther away. The "lift" was ancient, with manually operated doors, but it worked wonderfully. Large windows in our room faced the nice neighborhood below, providing a quiet, charming retreat for us both at the end of tiring days.

A few days after he returned from PT, he was clinging to my hand, whining, although I could tell he didn't require my support. When he saw the elevator, he let go and *ran* to it to be the first to open the door. Then he took three or four steps from the elevator to our door. When I pointed out to him that he walked without my help, he would not stop! He just kept going, from the table to the TV, to the bed, to the bathroom, over and over. I was as proud of him as he was of himself.

After a good night's rest, I was sure he'd be eager to show Mary his progress. On the way to the car, I let go of his hand, thinking he'd take off like he had in the hotel room. But his memory was short, and we were now outside. I stayed just beyond his reach, Ionut wailing in terror. He ran to grab my hand, which stayed inches in front of him. For two full car lengths, he kept going while wailing at the top of his lungs until his face was beet red. When I let him catch me for a hug, his little heart was pounding.

Everything the child did, he did with intensity. When I convinced him to take a deep breath and stop to think, only then did he realize that he was able to walk by himself. Amazed and pleased with himself, he continued to walk and walk all day. He wore me out practicing stopping, starting, turning around, getting up, and getting down. Mary had taught him well and prepared him to make all necessary moves.

The smug grin on his face as he strutted into PT spoke volumes as if to say, "What are you guys looking at? I knew I could do it all along!" When the day ended, he was discharged from their therapy, and follow-up services would continue once a week in Fond du Lac.

My prayer would match the writer of Proverbs:

> *My son, obey your father's commands,*
> *and don't neglect your mother's instruction.*
> *Keep their words always in your heart.*
> *Tie them around your neck.*
> *When you walk, their counsel will lead you.*
> *When you sleep, they will protect you.*
> *When you wake up, they will advise you.*
>
> PROVERBS 6:20–22, NLT

GROWING UP

Often, well-meaning friends would bring us articles or tell us stories about kids with disabilities who excelled in various sports. We treated our son the same as our other children, allowing and encouraging him to try whatever interested him—usually one thing at a time—so we would not be playing taxi driver continually. We avoided putting any pressure on him, however, to outperform other kids in the same activity. We wanted him to have the freedom to try without any expectations of performance. The goal was to have him be comfortable in his own skin and confident enough to try whatever he wanted to. Over the years, he had fun with quite a variety of activities without becoming passionate or anxious about any of them.

Swimming. Early on, watching Noot splash about and enjoy his bath, I noted how much it calmed him down. Living in Wisconsin, where there are thousands of lakes, gave me an idea. Most children are enrolled in swimming lessons for safety purposes, but I thought it would be something active that he would really enjoy. At the local YMCA, older teens and college students typically taught the little ones to swim, so I was not surprised that was the case when I took him for his first lesson.

Parents were to watch from behind a glass wall. Before long, a young college student had the little ones splashing about near the side of the pool as she demonstrated blowing bubbles underwater, then advancing to treading water while being supported by a noodle float. Oddly, though, she simply carried Noot on her hip while she worked with the other five or six children.

If this was repeated at the next lesson, I was prepared to ask her privately why she did that, but older, more experienced teacher Jacquie Nett was at the next lesson. To my delight and Noot's, she helped him do whatever she expected the other children to try. After the lesson, I thanked her for believing in him and asked if she would be teaching the class. Though she was only a sub for the day, she told me she had instructed many children with all kinds of disabilities and offered to give him private swim lessons, which we quickly arranged.

Within a couple of weeks, under Jacquie's patient tutelage, Noot was able to swim across the pool unassisted without a life jacket. Loving the freedom of movement that the water provided, he became an excellent swimmer. We would later move to a home with a backyard pool and enjoyed many summer afternoons watching Noot, his friends, and his niece and nephews swim and play water games.

Wrestling. When he was in first or second grade, there was a junior wrestling program through the recreation department. Wrestling would be another activity he could try without the awkward prosthetics. He was quite strong and muscular for his age and learned the moves quickly. The coach was quick to notice that the other boys his size avoided being paired with him to practice. One day he had them circle around as he brought out two pennies—one shiny and the other dark and dull. He asked the kids which one was worth more. Noting that they understood, he explained that the same is true of people. Although we may look different, we all have the same value. His own son was Noot's most frequent partner. Although Noot was a year or two older, they were about the same weight. Because the lad was younger, Noot usually let him win.

Biking. Throughout the years, we hosted guests from all over the country in Dixon House Bed and Breakfast. Richard S. and his girlfriend, Diane, were guests in October 1999, part of a motorcycle rally. Richard, an engineer, was quite impressed with Ionut's enthusiasm and willingness to try anything. They both had adventurous and boisterous personalities, and they really hit it off. Just before Christmas, Richard returned with a three-wheeled bike for Ionut. Rather than a typical bike with training wheels, he had designed this one with two rear wheels as large as the front one. Yet it was not like a typical trike either. He had designed the handlebars and pedals to work for Noot's limbs of different lengths.

Living on a farm with a long, paved driveway, Noot made many rounds on our circled driveway in the summers ahead. Although Richard had made sure it was not too small and he would not outgrow it, he really wanted to try a two-wheeled bike.

Enter Richard K. In 2004, another engineer was in town with a truckload of bikes of all kinds, willing to instruct kids with a variety of challenges to ride two-wheelers. After enlisting and training several enthusiastic volunteers to help, Richard K. invited the kids to try learning to ride a bike. Another Richard knew what adjustments to make, and a volunteer did indeed help Ionut to ride a two-wheeler without training wheels. It appeared that men with the name "Richard" were destined to be in Ionut's path.

Scooter. After the farm, we lived in a small subdivision with neighbors, which meant other children for Noot to play with. While they enjoyed the pool in the summer, there were dozens of spring and autumn days too chilly for that. We discovered that his favorite way to get around the neighborhood with the others was on a scooter. Steering the front wheel with the upright handle and propelling with his left foot, he could keep up with them and never felt left out.

Windsurfing. During one of his theater performances, Ionut was noticed by Kevin, who owned a windsurfing rental and instruction business on the shore of Lake Winnebago. He very excitedly offered to teach Ionut to windsurf, giving him free personal lessons and using his equipment. Ionut thought, *Why not? Sounds like fun*!

Kevin chose a day with light winds to start the lessons. I brought a lawn chair and sat to watch with a pair of prosthetic legs beside me on the grass. I brought them with me for several lessons until Ionut was able to also master the windsurfing on his own. Kevin was the most thrilled at being able to teach him. When the days became cooler, along with the water, the lessons ended, and by the following summer, Noot was on to other things.

Drama and Music. Intensity and drama are two characteristics of high-spirited kids, so I decided to put those to use by enrolling Ionut in children's chorale and children's theater. He seemed to enjoy both—even more than the physical activities. He still had the good strong musical voice that attracted the attention of surprised chorus directors. *Guys and Dolls Jr*, *Fiddler on the Roof*, and *Wizard of Oz* are a few of the musicals he performed with his peers.

In middle school, he learned to play a baritone but lost interest after the first year. In high school, he sang in chorus groups. Having a rich baritone voice, he won first place in the state solo and ensemble competition, singing "Gia il sole dal Gange." It was our privilege to be at home whenever he would practice.

Looking back, there seemed to be a recurring theme of favorites. He loved putting things in a backpack or wheeled luggage and pretending to go on a trip. Both were frequently filled with toys and assorted items as he would schlep them around the house and down the driveway taking imaginary journeys. He also used multiple objects like microphones—hairbrushes, forks, sticks—as he spoke loudly or sang into them. I recall coming into his room to find all of his stuffed animals lined up in rows on the bed like an audience while young Noot "preached" a funeral service to them. *Airplanes*—and anything having to do with airplanes or airports—were his passion. Fortunately, we traveled by air multiple times while he was growing up, so this was easy to discover.

Ionut was invited to tell his adoption story to countless groups of children and youth while he was growing up. Never bashful in front of a "crowd," he spoke to school classes (not his own) and Sunday school classes and youth groups, describing his adoption and his use of prosthetics. He would always explain to listeners how they, too, could be adopted by God the Father. He used a simple acronym to understand:

A Admit you are a sinner, as we all miss the standard set by a holy God. "For all have sinned and fall short of the glory of God" (Romans 3:23).

B Believe that Jesus, who is the Son of God, paid for your sin through His death and resurrection from the dead. "For it is by believing in your heart that you are made right with God, and it is by openly declaring your faith that you are saved" (Romans 10:10, NLT).

C Choose to accept Jesus' payment for your sin and then follow Him in obedience.

"Today I have given you the choice between life and death, between blessings and curses. Now I call on heaven and earth to witness the choice you make. Oh, that you would choose life, so that you and your descendants might live! You can make this choice by loving the LORD your God, obeying him, and committing yourself firmly to him. This is the key to your life. And if you love and obey the LORD, you will live long" (Deuteronomy 30:19–20, NLT). "So now we can rejoice in our wonderful new relationship with God because our Lord Jesus Christ has made us friends of God" (Romans 5:11, NLT).

While only a high school freshman, he shared his story at a United for Life fundraising dinner in the Fox Valley, where about 800 guests gave him a standing ovation. We all stand by to see how God will guide him to use his gifts.

How beautiful are the feet of those who bring good news.

ROMANS 10:15

ROMANIAN PASTORS AND WISCONSIN STORMS

During the 1990s, our church supported a missionary to Romania. At the invitation of Steve Farina, Pastor Tim Haugen and a small team traveled to Bucharest in early 1998 to teach pastors recently liberated from communism a method of church planting. This was based on home groups of new followers of Christ learning from their pastors how to discover and develop their spiritual gifts. These Romanian pastors were on fire for the Lord and welcomed all Christian literature and theological instruction. Pastor Gavin Moldovan of Cluj, Napoca, accepted an invitation to Wisconsin to learn more and discuss a partnership between our church and the fledgling Romanian evangelical churches.

I recall a private conversation with Gabi, telling him what was on my heart. Anticipating our adoption of a Romanian child whose parents we would never meet, I was delighted to know that the gospel was being spread throughout a country still blighted by communism and the suppression of Christianity. Although Romanian Orthodox was known as the religion of the region, it seemed based on ritual and tradition, having a form of religion, but lacking a personal relationship with God through His Son, Jesus Christ. The growing enthusiasm to plant evangelical churches gave me hope that our son's birth parents would one day hear the true good news. If never reunited on this earth, they could look forward to a reunion with their son in heaven if they understood the gospel and embraced their salvation through Jesus Christ.

Pastor Ken Nabi became involved in the partnership and led another team to continue the development of church planting in Romania. He really connected with Pastor Mihai Dumitrascu of Galati, and they formed a personal relationship that continues to this day. Their friendship and the partnership between our church and Biserica Emanuel continue to thrive.

When Mihai came to visit Wisconsin in 2000, our family was given the privilege of hosting him. By then, Ionut was a happy camper and always gregarious. He loved having Mihai there in the evenings and entertaining him with his antics and games. Mihai likes to tell the story of Noot bouncing and jumping around on the couch and running all over the house on his knees or crawling fast without his prosthetics. Mihai expected him to either wear the prosthetics all the time or just sit around when they were off.

My favorite story about his visit happened in the middle of the night. It had been a sultry, stormy evening, and we all retired early. We were awakened by a siren. Ron and I knew immediately that it was a tornado warning. He grabbed Ionut and went to the basement, and I knocked on Mihai's door to let him know that we had to go to the basement. He must have heard the siren, too, as he was already awake. He followed us calmly to the basement, where we would sit on folding chairs in our pajamas. You must understand that we lived in a century-old farmhouse. This was not a nice, finished basement like modern houses have. It was a cellar with foundation walls of fieldstone and low, exposed ancient wooden beams that held up the floors above us. Ron and Mihai both had to duck to avoid hitting their heads on these bare beams. An enormous furnace, water heater, and other assorted mechanicals occupied the majority of the damp, small space, while cobwebs hung from the corners. Fortunately, we had grabbed a flashlight and battery-operated radio on our way down, for the power soon went off.

In perfect English, Mihai asked, "What is a tornado?" When we explained, he told us they do not have those in Romania. A decade later, when Noot and I visited him in Galati, he informed me of a tornado in Wisconsin, which he had seen on the internet. It happened to be in Platteville, my hometown. You can't make this stuff up!

Years later, Mihai was again in Wisconsin. Scheduled to preach at our church on Sunday, April 17, 2015, he was our guest in our current home, with a nicely finished basement. That third weekend in April, a blizzard developed with a fury. At least twelve inches of heavy wet snow fell with blinding winds all of Saturday and on into Sunday. For the first time ever, our in-person church service was canceled. Adam Utecht, our savvy young pastor, arranged and set up for Mihai to preach via the internet from our home library.

I would hurry to my place of refuge from
the stormy wind and heavy gale.

PSALM 55:8, NASB

THE OTHER MOTHER

Throughout the years, Noot would have the typical difficulties of any adolescent as he sorted out life and looked for his own identity. We never tried to hide his adoption from him or anyone else. He had an incredibly good memory, making it impossible to hide anything from him, even if we wanted to—which we didn't. When he asked questions, we responded with the truth, appropriate for his age and capacity for understanding. We kept key information within our family, ensuring he did not hear any facts from others before he heard them from us.

Fortunately, we knew that his birth parents were married, and he was wanted. We also knew that there was no explanation for his birth anomalies. His mother had not taken any substance that would have caused them. His father had completed background health information to the degree that it was known to him.

One question that came up for Ionut from time to time was, "I just wonder what they look like?" To that, I would say, "Look in the mirror. You must look just like one of them—very handsome."

Although he pretended to be satisfied, we both knew he really was not.

Noot called me from college in Wilmore, Kentucky, in November to wish me a happy birthday and announce the good news.

"I found my birth parents!"

He went on to describe how he had searched social media for his last name, Stoica. Finding an abundance with that surname, he added the first names we had provided earlier. Not wanting to intrude or shock them, he contacted their daughter first. When she responded quickly, he asked several key questions, which she was able to verify. She was not shocked at all, as her parents had not kept his birth or adoption a secret from her either.

Andreea, thrilled to inform her parents about this connection, verified that they, too, were excited to hear from Ionut. With the help of translation apps, communication began to flow intermittently between all of us.

Looking at Andreea's picture was like seeing a female version of our son. Viewing the pictures of Carmen and Catalin was like seeing him twenty years into the future. At last, he was delighted to know what they looked like. Their loving and welcoming response to him was a relief to all of us.

As excited as he was, we did ask him to wait until his graduation to plan a visit. We all needed time to process, pray, and plan for that unforgettable experience. For now, it was deeply gratifying for Ionut to know what they looked like and that he did indeed "look like them."

For nothing is hidden, except to be revealed; nor has anything been secret, but that it would come to light.

Mark 4:22, NASB

WEDDING INVITATION

Graduation from Asbury University with a degree in media communications was a great accomplishment for Noot. Immensely proud of him, we made it a family celebration, driving down to Kentucky with Aaron, his wife, and their three children. His sister Kara flew from Seattle to attend. Our hearts were full as we recalled his humble beginnings, and his life achievements passed like a film before our eyes. Most of the orphans from St. Parascheva's would be uneducated and unprepared for life as adults, and the endless cycle of begging and street life of drugs would be the future for many. Here was that boy who was once an orphan, graduating from college with a bright future ahead of him, soaring like an eagle. Regarding the future, the heart of an orphan believes he must fight for whatever he can get while the heart of sonship is released to his inheritance.

Noot stayed in touch with his birth sister Andreea privately through social media messaging. Early in the year 2019, she informed him of her engagement to Christi Andries. She and her parents invited him—and yes, us—to her wedding in July. Excited to meet them all, we accepted the invitation and made flight reservations. This trip would be our graduation gift to our son, fulfilling our promise to him. Thankful to God for opening all the doors, we would trust Him with the details.

Meanwhile, Eugen and Nicoleta Iordache visited us in Wisconsin in April. Eugen was one of the pastors at the Biserica Emanuel in Galati, which we supported. (His wife, Nico, is Pastor Mihai's sister.) This would be their first visit to the US, and we were eager to host them. Ionut and I had last seen them in 2014 when we took a trip to Galati. He was nineteen at the time, and we wanted him to visit the country and experience the language and culture of his birth. That experience had been enriching for him, tasting, smelling, and hearing the surroundings that nourished his roots.

Noot again traveled alone to Timisoara, Romania, in 2016 to spend the summer with missionary friends of ours. Harriet and Steve were running a camp for children and youth of the Roma culture—a minority population otherwise known as Gypsies—in Romania. During those weeks, he developed an appreciation for the remarkable differences in cultures. At the same time, he could see that the universal need for all people is intimacy with God.

Now, in 2019, God used those experiences to help us weave together a reunion with Ionut's birth parents. While spending time in our home, Eugen inquired how he could help us with our plans. We were comfortable enough flying into Bucharest, but from there, we knew it would be awkward, not knowing the language and being so unfamiliar with big cities and public transportation. He was quick to open their home in Galati to us for a few days on either side of the wedding in Huşi, a town unfamiliar to us. In classic Romanian hospitality, he also offered to provide all the ground transportation. Nico was confident that their son, Octavian, known to us as Tavi, could be our translator while spending time with Ionut's other family.

Wanting to be sensitive to Carmen and Catalin's feelings, I began to prepare a gift for them. Searching through the years of my multitudes of photos, I selected many to tell the story of their son's childhood and years growing up in Wisconsin. Some were adventures and achievements, but most were ordinary days. Ionut and I reviewed them together, planning the layout and verbiage for a photo book to be ordered online and printed for them. In addition, we asked Tamara Neacsu, another Galatian friend, to translate a written version of my dream and Ron's "letter from God" for them.

Share with the saints in their needs; pursue hospitality.

ROMANS 12:13, CSB

What he opens no one can shut, and
what he shuts no one can open.

ISAIAH 22:22

STANDBY FOR GALATI

In Galati, Pastor Mihai Dumitrascu and the others at Emanuel Biserica were thrilled to know that Ionut would meet his parents. Many orphans from the nineties had been adopted into other countries, but happy reunions were uncommon. They told us story after story of unhappy, even ugly, endings. The public propaganda news media enjoyed relaying the worst of those. I'd always noticed that perpetrators of evil like to portray adoption as not only bad but even sinister. Knowing that fact, I'd always prayed that God would close the doors to a reunion if it would not be pleasant for Ionut. I'd asked Him to make a way and open the doors only if it would be pleasing to Him and uplifting to all involved. He had opened door after door.

Pastor Mihai invited us to come and tell our story to his home group of several adults who studied the Bible together. Those hearing it were moved to tears, and men spoke words of gratitude to our son for explaining how wonderful God is. One man exhorted him to become a preacher.

We were invited to tell it again during the Sunday service. Ionut did not hold anything back as he described his journey and upcoming reunion. One lady, Mariana Constantin, recalled having heard of him and seeing him as a baby on the news back in 1995, the year he was born. She had seen a newspaper article and a TV story twenty-four years ago about a baby who was born without feet, and she was certain that our son was that same child! She asked if he might be willing to share his story now as an adult with the media again. She pointed out that it would encourage Romanians about the redemptive power of God.

Out of consideration for the privacy of Ionut's birth family, we wanted time to prayerfully consider that. If the time should ever become right, we believed God would let us know.

Pastor Mihai also invited Ionut to return the following Sunday to share about the coming reunion. We left that invitation open, depending on how it all turned out and what his emotions and energy level would be.

Oh give thanks to the Lord; call upon his name;
make known his deeds among the peoples!

Psalm 105:1, ESV

FAMILY REUNION

Two days before the wedding, feeling incredibly blessed, I stepped out the door of Nico and Eugen's home for a walk before anyone else awoke. I started to the left, and toward the busy highway stood lovely greenhouses covering acres of beautiful geraniums, begonias, petunias, and multitudes of other blooming delights. Then I went back and beyond Iordache's house and down the hill. I noticed the lovely homes behind all the fences—some fancy, others merely functional.

Occasionally, I paused to collect a pretty rock. Once, as I did, I noticed an old man behind a fence enclosing a beautiful garden of hollyhocks, fruit trees, tomatoes, chickens, and turkeys. I wondered how long he had been watching me as he smoked his pipe and smiled. If only I knew Romanian, I would have paused for a friendly chat.

When I returned, Nico served us a wonderful breakfast. She had made ham and cheese sandwiches, tomato salad, and a second salad of fresh fruit from their orchard. After enjoying it leisurely, we packed up to be ready for the ride later to Huşi (pronounced *Hoosh*).

Excitement was building as we were about to be a part of a story God was writing, one we could not author on our own. We decided to meet his family a couple days prior to the ceremony, so his sister could be the rightful center of attention on her wedding day.

The Stoica family had graciously arranged hotel rooms in Huşi for all of us. The two-hour drive through the eastern rural areas of Moldova County would be absolutely soothing in its simplicity.

Before lunch, there was time for Nico to take us shopping at a new mall. Stores were large, wide open, and brightly lit. The mezzanine was tiled in very shiny white tile and adorned with bright chandeliers. We easily found dress attire for Noot to wear to his sister's wedding. Eugen picked us up in a seven-passenger Dacia he had borrowed for the road trip to Huşi. Besides driving, he was a good tour guide and took copious photos and videos of this once-in-a-lifetime occasion.

Nico outdid herself, preparing and serving us a "last lunch" at her table. She served us chicken, pork, potatoes seasoned with paprika, broccoli, fruit salad, and lemonade.

Eugen and Tavi loaded the micro-minivan, and Nico graciously found her way to the third row so Ron, Noot, and I could sit shoulder to shoulder behind Eugen and Tavi. At 2:30 p.m., we were on the road to discover the answers to Ionut's years of unanswered questions.

In just a few minutes, we were going north in the country, covering hills and valleys of farmland. Fields of sunflowers, wheat, and corn were at various stages of growth and harvest. Farmers worked with ancient equipment or only a horse, some even forking straw into piles by hand. Shepherds tending their flocks of sheep were a reminder of Jesus, our Shepherd. It was not uncommon to see a horse-drawn wagon load of straw, hay, or humans, for that matter. The tiny villages bustled with people going about their activities of daily living.

Eugen pointed out that we were in Vaslui County, which he considered to be the poorest area in all of Romania. Huşi, located on the northern border of Vaslui County, is seen from the side of a ridge—when approached from the south—and overlooks the city of approximately 38,000 residents. This view reminded us of approaching Fond du Lac from the Niagara Escarpment.

Eugen's GPS led him into the heart of the valley city where the Hotel Cantemir was located. The Stoica family had graciously provided hotel rooms for all of us there. As soon as the car was parked and we all climbed out for a stretch, we were surrounded immediately by Andreea, Christi, Carmen, Catalin, and Georgiana, another sister. The welcoming greetings and hugs were profoundly warm and speechless as everyone was at a loss for words. Tears of joy and relief flowed freely. The common language of all was love and joy.

After registering and dropping off our luggage, the Stoica family walked us to a beautiful nearby restaurant where we could all get acquainted over a lovely meal. Dinner began with everyone raising their glasses in a toast to this miraculous reunion. There were so many conversations going on at once that it was hard to comprehend it all. Everyone seemed so joyful, and there was so much to catch up on.

Ionut learned through Tavi that he was very much wanted and loved. We also learned how their hearts were broken as the Romanian Orthodox priest had advised them to relinquish him in hopes of a better life that adoption could offer him. The conditions in their area at the time were not such that they could find and acquire adequate medical care and prosthetics for him. Carmen herself was adopted and had worked in the field of adoption as a social worker, so she completely understood their heart-wrenching decision.

A year after his birth, they were blessed with a daughter, Andreea. Her birth was difficult, however, and Carmen was told she could not give birth safely again. A few years later, they adopted Georgiana. Since they loved children and grieved releasing their son, it was their way of expanding their family—and paying forward what someone had done for him.

Overnight, Ionut became part of the family of his origins. He would soon discover how large and loving that family was. As for me, I felt honored and blessed to be a player in this unfolding story of God's redeeming love and reconciliation. No longer was I watching a miracle from the front row, as I had done so many years ago, working at Bethany. Now I was humbled to be in a supporting role in the drama.

And we know that in all things God works for the good of those who love him, who have been called according to his purpose.

ROMANS 8:28

IONUT'S SOCIAL MEDIA ANNOUNCEMENT

Along with multiple pictures, Noot posted this greeting on social media:

> "Greetings from Romania. Many of you knew for a long time that I was adopted. Many of you also knew for a long time I wanted to find my birth family in Romania. I flew to Romania on July 7 with the intent to reunite with my sister, Andreea-Simona Stoica, who would marry Cristi Andries on Saturday with God's help. All glory be to Him! Today, July 11, 2019, I can proudly say I extended my family. I have reunited with my birth family. I am proud to be a member of the Stoica-Kuhls family. Thank you to everyone for supporting my

> families and me along the way. We could not have done it without your help. This is only the beginning of an incredible journey. Special thank you to Barbara Kuhls, Ronald Kuhls, Catalin and Carmen Stoica, Aaron Kuhls, and others for the help making this trip possible with transportation, lodging, and translation. Everything happens for a reason, and it makes us stronger as individuals and together as a whole! Never underestimate the power of adoption!"

To his surprise, that post was commented on 66 times and liked by 381 followers.

What I tell you in darkness, tell in the light; and what you hear whispered in your ear, proclaim on the housetops.

MATTHEW 10:27, NASB

LUNCH ON THE FARM

Ionut's "Stoica family" invited us to have a meal with them at their home in the country one day before the wedding. Feeling very honored and blessed, we enjoyed the thirty-minute ride to their farm. As Eugen easily drove past fields of sunflowers, vineyards, tiny villages, and pastures again, Ionut spoke quietly to me about his observations of the contrast between this land, the people, culture, and what he was used to in Wisconsin. He understood and appreciated the best of both.

When Eugen turned off the twenty-first-century, state-of-the-art road onto a tiny gravel road, Ron and I looked at each other with question marks in our eyes. It soon became no more than a tractor lane going uphill to a typical Romanian farm. Another car had just arrived, and a middle-aged Romanian couple stepped out of their car, chattering loudly to the farm's occupants. Carmen and Catalin were excited to greet and embrace their son again, and we all felt their warm, enthusiastic welcome.

It was a very warm July day, so instead of going inside, we were all ushered onto a porch. There, an exceptionally long homemade table, covered with a rose-patterned tablecloth, was set with fine china for lunch. Nico gestured to me to follow her between the table and porch railing, where we sat on a long, narrow bench covered by a blanket. Ron followed, sitting next to me on the homemade bench. Eugen followed, still chatting in Romanian as introductions were made. As he sat, the bench began to crack, and we all jumped up immediately, laughing hysterically. Catalin and his cousin were quick to remove that bench and replace it with another identical one from the yard before we could even stop laughing. Eugen then sat on a stool opposite us, refusing to join us on the new bench as we all continued to laugh.

Catalin was quick to bring us an assortment of beverages, and we all raised our glasses in a toast to this marvelous reunion. In the utmost of Romanian hospitality, peanuts and snacks were brought to us as other guests, all family members, arrived. Dishes of roasted rabbit, seasoned potatoes, and homemade pickles appeared and quickly disappeared as we dined, discussed, and laughed. For dessert, Sylvia—the wife of Catalin's cousin—brought a cheesecake type of pastry from Bucharest, where they live.

Before we were finished eating, Andreea, Christi, and Georgiana returned from Huşi, where they were finalizing wedding details. With their help and Tavi's, we managed to communicate as we attempted to fill in so many gaps in Ionut's history.

After lunch, Christi invited us to see his rabbits. There, we saw the earthy side of the farm as he proudly showed us the hutches filled with large rabbits and cubs just recently born. Opening a hutch, he reached in and handed Ionut a large hare to hold and pet. This brought back memories of my own brother raising rabbits for food when I was a child. At our feet, chickens pecked at the ground for insects and scattered chicken feed.

Ionut's birth aunt Sylvia served coffee on the porch, where we had the honor to meet his elderly grandmother. She could not take her eyes off him and held his hand in hers for quite a spell as she gazed into his eyes with approval. I greeted her too, and language was not a problem as we communicated with hugs, smiles, and our eyes.

After taking many photos and some very long goodbyes, we departed, knowing they still had much to do before Andreea and Christi's big day. As for us, we continued north to the city of Iasi, where Ionut was born.

To know where one is going, it is usually helpful to know where one came from. Carmen and Catalin lived in Iasi at the time of Ionut's birth. Although we were unable to locate the hospital, and the orphanage no longer existed, at least we were in the city of his birth. We visited the central park, where we had taken him in a stroller with Gabi in 1998. Although our memories were of winter, it was nice to see the same park blooming with flowers and lush shade on this summer day. Statues and walkways were familiar to us all.

After a little more sightseeing and shopping, we dined in a very elegant restaurant called La Cupola within a mall across the street. We each noticed the contrast between the settings of our lunch and dinner. All agreed that the casual, family atmosphere of lunch was the favorite. We enjoyed a quiet, long sunset drive back to Huşi as we each became lost in our thoughts and exhaustion.

There is nothing better for a person than to eat, drink, and enjoy his work. I have seen that even this is from God's hand.

Ecclesiastes 2:24, CSB

WEDDING DAY

From our hotel window, we could see that Christi and his friends were decorating their cars with lavender netting and flowers. Eugen drove Ionut back to the Stoica farm, where the Romanian Orthodox pre-wedding festivities began. Eugen sent us a video so we could view quite a bit of this fun, all new to us Americans.

The wedding party arrived at the gate where Christi was required to pay to enter. Ascending the walkway, accompanied by his friends, he had to pay again before he was allowed to look upon his bride. Her Aunt Silvia was at the doorway, insisting loudly that he must pay more! All the while, musicians accompanied the festivities with loud, joyful music on saxophone and accordion. Once he, playing along, reluctantly paid again, the "bride" emerged, wrapped in lace from the crown of her head to her shoulders above a wedding gown. While the loud music continued, the veil was slowly removed to reveal it was really a boy in a bridal gown. They all exploded with hilarious laughter as more celebration and music followed.

There, Ionut was greeted by many more cousins, aunts and

uncles, and his paternal grandmother. They ate snacks and raised glasses to toast this celebration of a simultaneous reunion and wedding.

After our leisurely lunch with Nico and Tavi, Ron and I dressed for the wedding. Eugen and Noot returned just in time to take us all to the orthodox church, just a five-minute drive away from the ceremony. Being the last to enter, we were surprised to find everyone standing in the small building. Four priests were already chanting and singing as everyone, including the bride, groom, wedding party, and parents, all faced them and the altar.

The sight of Andreea, the beautiful bride, was breathtaking. Everyone was dressed in their finest, but she outshined them all, holding a tall white candle adorned with an elegant bouquet of red roses and white camellias. The lace bodice and cap sleeves of her gown descended to a flowing long full skirt of lace over silk. Without her glasses, everyone could see the love in her eyes.

One priest, while chanting, solemnly placed gold crowns on Andreea and Christi. The chanting and singing continued throughout the ceremony as they exchanged vows and rings, and the priests shook copious amounts of incense all around, over and over. Georgiana needed to step out and get some fresh air when the incense and stuffiness inside began making her queasy.

Another priest served communion to the wedding party. At this point, we expected them to kiss and proceed out of the church. To our surprise, the priests then joined hands with everyone in the wedding party, and they danced in a circle around the altar as the priests continued to sing. Following a brief message to the couple, tiny cookies and cups of soda were served to the few remaining guests. Standing for well over an hour in the heat of the small unventilated room had already forced a number of guests to retreat outside.

Inside the venue, professional photographers recorded the event for the bridal couple. Along with family members and other guests, we were also taking cell phone pics for our own memories of this joyous occasion. Dozens of us were outside by then, snapping photos between conversations and embraces.

As the wedding couple emerged from the church, ushers emptied two buckets of water on the walk at their feet to bless them. Fellowship and congratulations continued until everyone was in their cars to drive away. There would be a break for a few hours until the reception later that evening. What no one told us was that all the ladies would change out of their beautiful dresses into even more formal wear. Exhausted and hearts full of sensory overload, we took a nap.

Leaving the hotel later, we met the Iordaches in the lobby. Eugen was talking to some of Catalin's family members. His brother's wife and another couple traveled from Norfolk, England, where they lived. She had a picture to show Ionut. The image was of a lady she knew who worked in St. Parascheva's when he was there. He did indeed recall her after looking at her picture briefly! God had ensured that loving souls would look after him throughout his time there, praying for his future.

The reception hall, Omnia Venue, was close by, so we walked to the reception, which was to begin at 8:00 p.m. Arriving well after that hour, we were practically the first guests there! Outside, the hosts handed us glasses of champagne to toast the bride and groom as we entered. Christi ushered us warmly to a table where Andreea's parents would also sit, although they were up and greeting others more than they sat. The entire hall and tables were decorated with exceptional elegance. Tables were set with fine china, multiple beverage choices, and a cake pedestal draped and piled high with fruit, nuts, desserts, rolls, cheese, and other fancy hors d'oeuvres.

Music included a pleasant variety of American dance, interrupted often by the loud and jocular folk jingle that announced the arrival of more guests. When the sax and accordion started, the wedding couple immediately stopped dancing and ran to the door to greet and warmly welcome the new guests. That continued until the last guests arrived.

At 10:00 p.m., plates of fancy, bite-sized appetizers were served. The merriment continued as live romantic music began, to which the bridal couple danced while light and smoke machines captured everyone's attention. The music again became livelier, and more couples joined them on the dance floor in their formal wear.

While this continued, Ionut was introduced to group after group of extended family members and friends, who shared warm, enthusiastic embraces. The shoulders of his white shirt were pleasantly stained with makeup from so many female tears of joy.

Although the celebration would continue all night, we began our goodbyes. In the Romanian culture, these were prolonged and included copious last photos and hugs. Well after 11:00 p.m., we began our walk back to Hotel Cantemir with hearts too full to recognize our exhaustion. Ionut was unable to contain his satisfaction and delight. Watching our son's heart filled was a mother's dream come true.

Be devoted to one another in love. Honor one another above yourselves.

ROMANS 12:10

WITNESS TO THE ASSEMBLY

As agreed the previous night, we were all in the car by 6:30 a.m. and on the way south to Galati. Around 7:30, we stopped in a small town for coffee and snacks. Processing all the events from the wedding day, we laughed about the things we did not understand. Mostly, though, we were all very thankful that Ionut—and all of us—were so warmly welcomed.

We either dozed or daydreamed quietly while Eugen drove rapidly along the windy country roads, determined to give us all time to clean up and eat before he took us to the 11:00 a.m. church service. I was again enchanted by the scenery, the small villages, and their inhabitants. Once, we found ourselves in a rural "traffic jam" of sorts. Just as Eugen attempted to pass a vehicle, a stray dog darted out while a pedestrian and bicyclist also appeared. He tooted the horn to warn the farmer not to enter the road on his horse-drawn wagon.

As a light rain began, I could no longer hold my eyes open. When I awoke minutes later, I recognized the streets of Galati.

Feeling accomplished, Eugen turned down his street at 9:30 a.m. Nico quickly prepared a proper breakfast while the rest of us changed our clothes.

Knowing we were Americans, Nico gave us headsets so we could hear most of the church service in English. The prayers were followed by exuberant worship, which gave me the feeling that I was standing among a choir of angels. Pastor Mihai then welcomed visitors, including us, then invited Ionut to the microphone.

With Mihai translating, Ionut shared the events of the past few days. True to form, he was comfortable with the microphone, highlighting all the important things clearly while keeping it brief. All became silent as they listened and wept tears of wonder at a God who loves so much. Ionut was warmly greeted and embraced often by everyone there. He received so much enthusiastic love and encouragement to continue telling his story. Some exhorted him to go into ministry and preach, telling all about the love of God.

As for his American parents, we were treated better than we deserved. Folks with wet cheeks embraced us and kissed us, blessing us. I could not have imagined the parents of a rock star being more warmly adulated. Even with the difference in language, it was made known to us that we were considered heroes and would always be welcomed back. The family wedding and this welcome seemed like a foretaste of being welcomed into our eternal home in the Father's house.

The whole assembly became silent as they listened.

Acts 15:12

BELIEVING THE UNBELIEVABLE

by the Stoica Family

Thinking readers would be interested in the perspective of Ionut's birth family, I received their support for this book. Following are their responses to questions we asked through Tamara Neacsu, our interpreter.

Let us know what you thought when you found out about Ionut through him contacting Andreea on social media.

The moment Andreea came to let us know that she was contacted by a boy requesting information about his birth, our thoughts flew to Ionut. Emotionally, we were in shock for a few weeks; we couldn't believe it—how it was possible that after so long, Ionut was alive, taking into consideration the chances he was given in hospital and how it was possible to find each other through social media.

We wanted to get in touch with him, but the feelings of remorse were growing. We didn't know what we could say to him; we didn't know what to start with and how to express everything we were feeling. We were happy that Ionuț was alive, that he was well, but also that there was a possibility for the siblings to meet and get to know each other.

We still thank God for making this meeting possible. We are deeply grateful for the possibility that has been given to us, that of a new beginning.

Were you nervous about inviting him and his American family to Andreea's wedding with all the extended family and friends who would be coming?

We were nervous; we didn't sleep for a few nights. We sat and talked every day; we didn't know what the meeting was going to be like, so we made a lot of scenarios. We wanted to give them some of our best.

There were two events with a strong emotional impact. The language barrier made it difficult, although even if we had been able to communicate in our mother tongue, we don't know how we would have managed to convey to him the regrets, the emptiness that has been left all this time, the uncertainties we have faced, the remorse we have had all these years.

The openness of Ionuț and his family left us deeply impressed, as well as the warmth and love with which they treated us and the way they handled the decision we made. The fact that we received understanding, compassion, and love from them left us deeply impressed.

Describe what it was like to finally see and embrace him again.

The moment we embraced him, we actually burst into tears; we couldn't believe that after so long, we had the opportunity to hug our child. There are no words to describe the joy that we felt. It was the most beautiful feeling; it was that feeling I had when I held him in my arms at birth. I felt that, finally, some of the wounds were healing and that God was finally preparing something good for us.

What were your thoughts about him over the years?

There have been years of uncertainty, of remorse. There were times when I stopped believing that there was a possibility that Ionuţ would live. Every time I looked at a family with children, with brothers and sisters, I felt an emptiness in my stomach and a lump in my throat. The fact that Ionuţ found us after so many years can only be considered a miracle.

Tell us about Georgiana's adoption.

We really wanted Andreea to have a little sister, so the desire to adopt was born. Following the birth of Ionuţ and the problems we faced, we fell into depression; the second pregnancy was somehow unconscious, given the fact that I had given birth by C-section and needed rest during the second pregnancy (Ionuţ was born on January 27, 1995, and Andreea on June 16, 1996; the distance between pregnancies was extremely small and the risk quite high).

The events that happened with Ionuţ—but also the fact that I, myself, was adopted—led us to adopt a child, to try to fill part of the existing gap.

Can you describe some of your work, Carmen, in adoption as a young adult?

In order to get into the system, I had to go through a schooling cycle, take a few courses, and pass a psychological assessment—both for myself and family members. I want to believe that I entered this field to find a refuge, find peace of mind, and feel that I was doing something useful for the community.

I always wanted a big family, lots of kids. I've always appreciated and looked at large, well-rounded families with some envy. Being able to make connections with a child who is not my own flesh and blood has helped me rediscover myself as a human being, as a woman, and not least as a mother.

Are you willing to write a bit about the advice you received about the heartbreaking decision to give up Ionuț for adoption?

The moment Ionuț was born and the doctors got in touch with his little deficiencies, they started doing a lot of tests and experiments on him. Unfortunately, we didn't have the opportunity to spend much time with him. When we were discharged, Ionuț was kept in the hospital for further investigations, and we were restricted from visiting him. After a series of tests and weeks spent in the hospital, we were informed that Ionuț would be placed in a foster home and that it would be best to go and sign the adoption papers.

We are not proud of the decision we made, but the moment we signed those papers, we thought we could give him a chance at a better future, a normal life. Unfortunately, we made the decision to give Ionuț up for adoption also under pressure from the families (my husband's and mine). We didn't have their support, and they failed to guide us to make a different decision.

We are aware that Ionuț's fate could have been *totally* different, but fortunately, God was generous with him and gave him a family where he had the opportunity to develop and learn what love, forgiveness, gratitude, and humility meant.

And we know that in all things God works for the good of those who love him, who have been called according to his purpose.

Romans 8:28

O'HARE AGAIN

It was six days before Thanksgiving, 2019. Ionut had been working as a customer service representative at a call center. Racing into the house full of excitement, he announced that he was to report for training at O'Hare International Airport the next morning! The call he had been waiting for sent his excitement level to a TEN.

He had limited hours to turn in his badge and equipment to Spectrum and plan his travel to Chicago from our home in the Fox Valley of Wisconsin. Reading the details of the emailed job offer to be prepared, he noticed "dress clothes required." Knowing that meant white shirts, neckties, black trousers, sport coat, and black shoes, it became a family team effort of rapid preparations.

While Noot gathered items to be returned to Spectrum, I took an inventory of his current wardrobe and found it severely lacking. I also called Romanian friends who live in Chicago. I began to describe the situation to Delia, noting that we did not know where he should go for temporary housing until he found an apartment. Before I could inquire about that, she knew where the conversation was going. "He can stay here with us," she declared. Details about the address, parking, and more soon followed.

Noot put a load of acceptable garments in the washing machine and then drove his Honda CRV to Spectrum to turn everything in. Armed with measurements and sizes, I headed off to accomplish my power shopping. Ron did what he does best while alone in the house—think and pray.

By the time we each had returned, Noot's clothes were in the dryer. I ripped tags off from garments, putting them in a quick washer cycle, attempting to remove wrinkles. I would also need to iron shirts and iron enforcement patches onto the insides of trouser legs. Without these, his pants become shredded from the inside out due to the constant catching of fabric in the back of his prosthetic knee.

By this time, early evening, Ron was trying to decide what time to drive Noot to the airport, with the intent to leave here around 4:00 a.m. to get him there (considering traffic) by 8:00 a.m. Hearing them discuss this, I didn't like it. Yes, my husband is an excellent driver with years of experience in long road trips, but the time of day was concerning to me. Nor did I like to consider our son driving yet that night, as was his plan. While a good and safe driver, his prosthetics make the effort of a long drive with congested traffic very tiring for him. This was not an effective way to begin a new job and make a first impression.

While they discussed it, I texted our older son, Aaron, to please come over and help problem solve. Arriving calmly a few minutes later, he made it simple. "I need to deliver something to Milwaukee tomorrow. I will drive Noot to Delia's house so he can drop off his luggage. Then I will take him to the airport. I can make my delivery to Milwaukee on my way back."

BAM! Problem solved. I made a decent meal and finished

packing for Noot. One-handed packing is laborious, and I really wanted him to rest. The chance that he would get adequate sleep was highly doubtful, however, considering how excited he was. Ron was a little relieved that Aaron would do the driving, considering all of it would be so early, and he was not a morning person. We all prayed. Comfortable in our beds, we did hear Aaron arrive, and the two of them departed hours before dawn.

Ionut continues to work in the airline industry and serves customers and employees in a most professional manner. He has worked for American Airlines, Envoy, and United. His favorite benefit, of course, is the free standby travel perk. Often, he will visit other airports and cities to explore them or meet up with friends. It is his dream to return to Romania and spend more time with his Stoica family, provided post-pandemic travel restrictions are ever lifted. Currently, he is scheduling flight crews for domestic flights. Stand by with us to watch where God will take him in the future.

The prudent understand where they are going.

PROVERBS 14:8, NLT

NOTES FROM THE AUTHOR

Send Me

The year was 1981. Completing a degree in nursing was challenging for most students. Already a wife and mother of two preschoolers had made it especially difficult for me, but I had accomplished it. By now, the children, ages nine and seven, were in school all day, and we were getting established as dairy farmers on eighty acres in Fond du Lac County. My husband, Ron, was a diligent worker who grew up on a farm, so he knew what he was doing.

Although I did what I could on the farm, my ability to earn extra income from nursing was the most useful to the family. After working a year in a medical-surgical unit, I landed the dream job in the obstetrics unit, witnessing and assisting the births of babies. As each tiny one emerged into the world and gasped their first breath, I knew I was witnessing a miracle. Assisting their new moms to find success in nurturing them taught me much about the uniqueness of each new creature. I also learned to appreciate the exceptional quality of each parent and sibling as they got acquainted with their new family member.

Many would celebrate the new life joining their families. Simultaneously others grieved the brief life of one they hoped and dreamed of. You see, not all babies survive birth and the neonatal period. Some are born too early and just cannot survive with even the best of care and medical technology. Others have severe birth anomalies that do not allow them to live long at all. Still others with less severe birth anomalies will have lifelong challenges not expected by their parents. Once I cared for a baby with anencephaly, his tiny head lacking a fully formed brain with only skin (no skull) to protect the contents of his head. His brief life touched many as his family and the staff did the best we could to care for him. Siblings came to visit, meet their new baby brother, hold him, and have family photos taken before their premature and sad goodbyes.

I held him until he breathed his last breath and carried him to the morgue with tears running down my own cheeks. I pondered the inconsistency of mourning the loss of those pregnancies while others were intentionally ending pregnancies through abortion at other locations.

During this season of life, I was simultaneously getting more serious as a follower of Christ.

I made a personal commitment to read the entire Bible in a year or less. Reading portions every day kept God often in my mind, so I found myself asking Him for answers to tough questions.

How can some be intentionally having their babies killed while others are longing for one and overcome with sorrow when theirs die naturally?

I began to understand that in the natural world, there is both good and evil. Everyone wants to make their own judgments about what is good and what is evil. I was learning that those judgments are not ours to make but God's alone. He was serious when He gave Moses the Ten Commandments, which included "Do not kill." The current use of euphemisms for abortion was only a deception used by some to justify killing others yet to be born. I came to know deeply that elective abortions were the killing of human life.

Reading the prophet Isaiah, I felt a personal calling, or commission, if you will.

Then I heard the voice of the Lord saying,
"Whom shall I send? And who will go for us?"
And I said, "Here am I. Send me!"
He said, "Go and tell this people."

Isaiah 6:8–9

I believed that He was telling me to be a voice for the voiceless, to speak up for those who could not speak for themselves.

Before attempting to speak up, I determined to educate myself with all the information I could find about the practice of abortion, the facts, statistics, and methods. I would also read everything I found that philosophized about the justification or the condemnation of it. I did not limit my investigation to religious information. I read everything I could find about the scientific and legal facts as well. I was horrified to learn that even several religious denominations found and devised rhetoric to defend the abhorrent practice. Reading the Bible gave me the perspective needed to discern truth from euphemistic rationalization. Real-life experiences in the obstetrics department confirmed my conclusions.

Opportunities soon presented themselves for me to speak up. Looking back, I wonder if they were tests to see if I would qualify to parent one more child—one *very special human being*. Our lives have been blessed and enriched by Ionut Georgian Stoica more than I can ever describe. We have met so many wonderful people that would have remained strangers to us if we had continued in our comfort zones, living our spoiled lives as empty nesters. The blessings far exceed any perceived sacrifices. One day he will tell his own stories, yet to unfold. God is writing your story as well. Be sure to show up for your own opportunities to be victorious over life's challenges.

I was not disobedient to the heavenly vision. To this day I have had the help that comes from God, and so I stand here testifying to both small and great.

Acts 26:19, 22, ESV

ADOPTION SCRAPBOOK

Power of a Dream

Mommy's Shoe

Learning to Swim

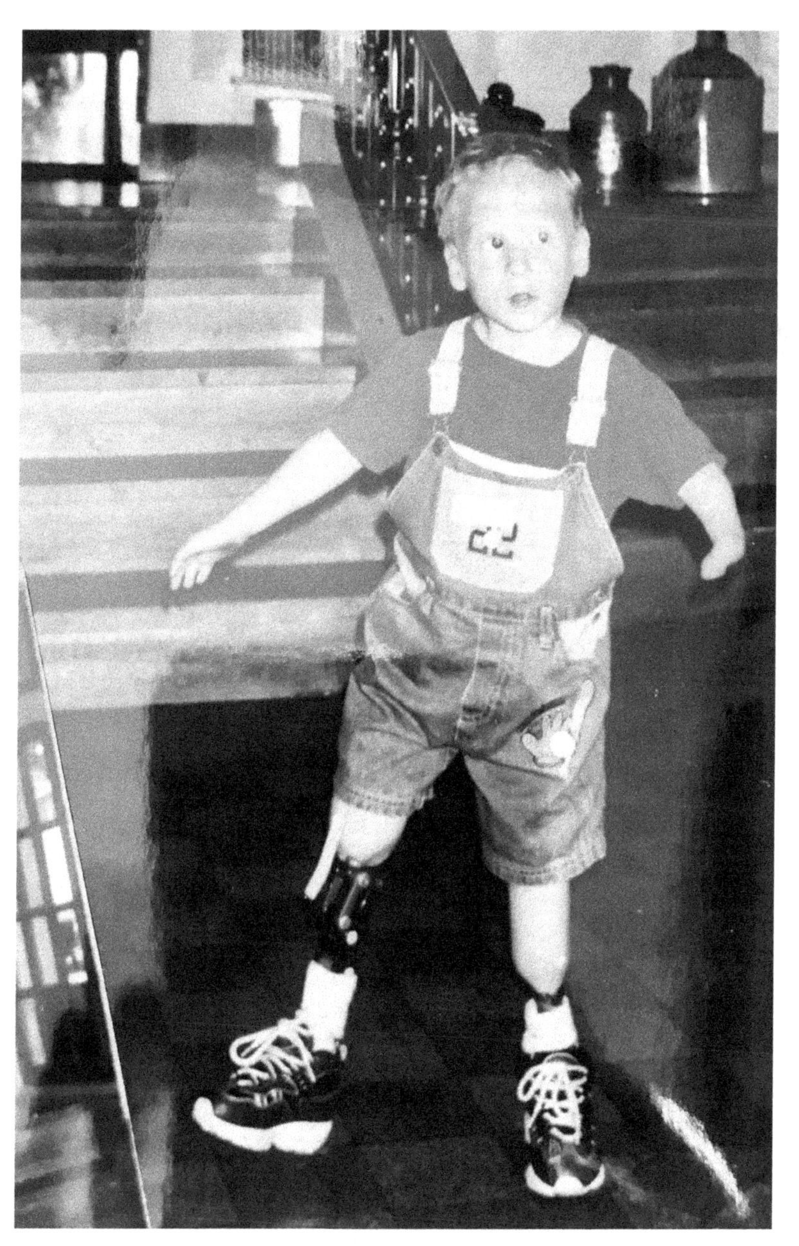

First Steps

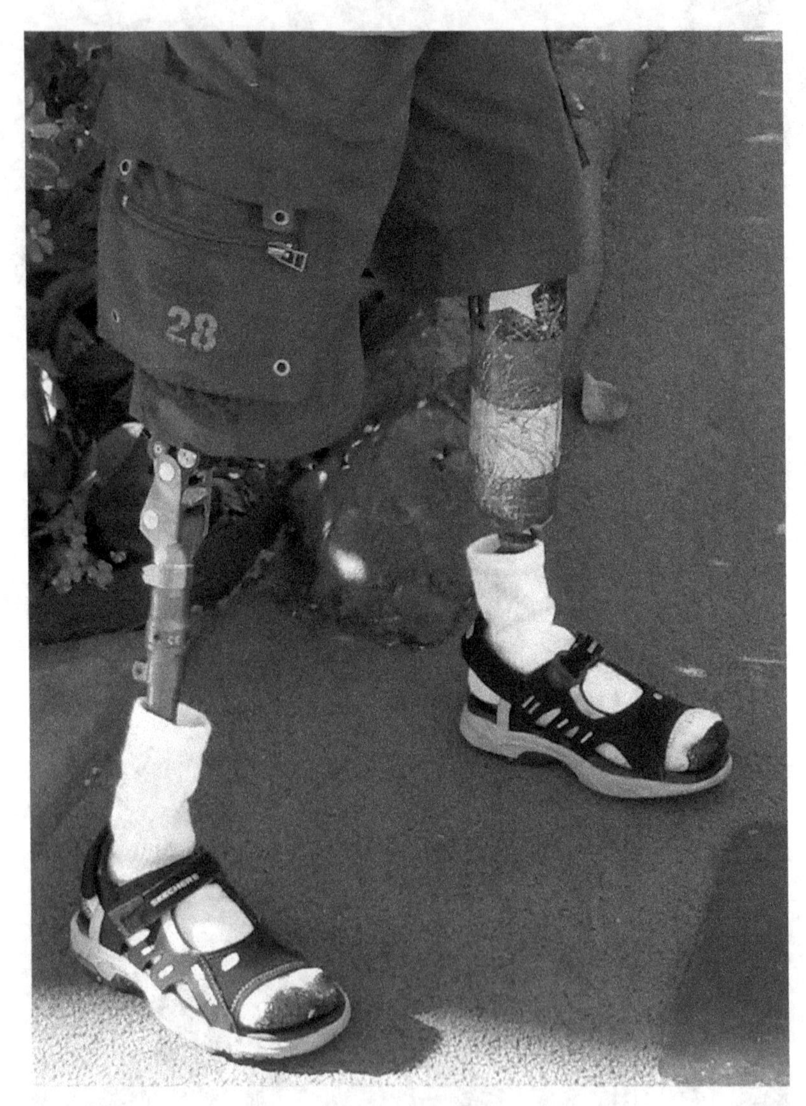

Beautiful Feet

Mom and Noot 2002

EAA 2005

Pastor Mihai and Ionut

Body Surfing in Maui

Fifth Grade Chorus

Middle School Band

Gramma Dorothy and Noot

Willis Tower 2013

Windsurfing

Noot, Nieces and Nephews 2008

Ionut, Nephew Sam, Niece Naomi

Ionut and Pastor Mihai

High School Graduation

Noot with Adoptive Parents

Pastor Eugen and Ionut

Portrait by a College Friend

Asbury Graduation

Asbury Diploma

Birthparents Catalin and Carmen Stoica with Son, Ionut

Andreea, Carmen, Ionut, Catalin Stoica

Wedding of Andreea and Christi Andries

ABOUT THE AUTHOR

Barbara is a registered nurse with a bachelor's degree in nursing from the University of Wisconsin, Oshkosh. She has over thirty years of experience in nursing, with that being divided between obstetrics, geriatrics/physical rehab, and endoscopy. Barbara established the Fond du Lac branch office of Bethany Christian Services Wisconsin, developing an advisory board and serving as a pregnancy counselor for five years. After retirement from paid positions, she continues to serve as a volunteer parish nurse for her church in Fond du Lac, Wisconsin.

Barbara lives in Wisconsin with her husband of over fifty years, Ronald. Together they raised two homegrown children and are blessed with six grandchildren. While she enjoyed the empty nest, they were hosts of the Dixon House Bed and Breakfast. Meeting people from all over the world and making new friends is her passion. When God called them to adopt another child, they knew that obedience was better than sacrifice. Ionut, their "bonus child," is the subject of this book. Both are retired now and enjoy traveling, gardening, and hosting guests again at Mahanaim, their home on

Lake Winnebago. (Look up Genesis 32:1–2 if you are curious about the name Mahanaim.) Barb still loves to read as much as possible, so you would not be surprised to find stacks of books shelved and strewn around her home and in her car. Her greatest joy is knowing Jesus, her very best friend.

CPSIA information can be obtained
at www.ICGtesting.com
Printed in the USA
JSHW052147061122
32715JS00001B/1

9 798218 046538